# TAKE THE LIMITS OFF YOUR FAITH

PROPHET ROGERS G. DECUIR

# Take the Limits off Your Faith

Prophet Rogers G. DeCuir

# Take the Limits off Your Faith

First Printing February 2020
Printed in the United States of America
ISBN: 978-0-578-65478-2

Published by:
Executive Business Writing
P.O. Box 10002
Moreno Valley, CA 92552
(951)268-0365
www.beverlycrockett.com
Editors: Dr. Beverly Crockett and Julie Boney
Transcribers: M. Darlene Carson – Sometime Virtual Assistant Services, and Tracy Spencer – Legacy Media, LLC
Cover design: Tracy Spencer

# Table of Contents

# Foreword

Dr. Rogers G. DeCuir has captured and embodied "super-action" faith for the Christian journey. Not fictitious or fantastic faith that is glorified but void of action and results. Rather, our author has put his finger on the pulse of lively, vivacious, and robust faith that, simply, gets the job done, resulting in victorious success for all who will read and become persuaded.

Abolish the frustration! Take the limits off your faith and become a part of this "next faith" community and experience the dynamic working power of God in real time.

No more fictitious faith that hypes but doesn't deliver. Instead, embrace the knowledge of the limitless faith outlined in this ingenious publication, and take your faith to the next level.

Dr. Joel McLeod
President
Next Dimension University

# Foreword

# Publisher's Note

I grew up in a season in which generals of the faith were on their post night and day, day and night. As I began to renew my walk with God as an adult, the power of God that I witnessed was phenomenal. Miracles were common. Healing and deliverance took place. There was a real move of God on the altar and throughout the church. Everything that I saw, I saw it manifest through the eyes of faith.

When that season of my life caused me to relocate to another part of the country, I longed to see those faith miracles in action. God sent a man of faith my way in the person of Prophet Rogers G. DeCuir. In this, his latest publication, *Take the Limits off Your Faith,* you will experience numerous firsthand accounts of Prophet DeCuir's teaching, preaching, prophesying, and leading the people of God through to manifesting their faith.

This book has been set up to take you behind the doors of the church into service after service. Most of the accounts are chronicled from taped sessions at various venues, and even include some from the powerful School of Faith that Prophet DeCuir has conducted.

You will not only hear and feel the power of God resonating through Prophet DeCuir, but you will be led to exercise your faith even more.

Prophet Rogers G. Decuir – a man of powerful FAITH. Though for some he has been ahead of his time, for many of us, through God, Prophet is right on time.

Take the limits off your faith and watch God move on your behalf.

Dr. Beverly Crockett
Executive Business Writing

# Acknowledgments

God bless you my friends. Certainly, I want to give special thanks to the many, many people who have helped me with this project. Thank God for those who prayed and stood with me.

I must give special thanks to my wife, Patricia, who prayed and encouraged me throughout this project. She continuously spoke words of faith to me that the project would come to fruition.

Additionally, I offer thanks to all of my children for the past 50 years as I have walked down through the avenue of faith ever since they were children. They were not aware of it, but they were walking down this avenue of faith with me. Now, many of them have grown up and they are walking down their own avenues of faith in the various fields in which God has assigned them.

Thank God for my daughter, Pastor Grace Decuir-Davidson, pastor of Holy Deliverance Church, which I pastored for over 50 years. I'm thankful that she had enough faith to accept that position, and I'm just amazed at how she demonstrates faith every day.

Thank God for my son, Jonathan DeCuir, who is such a man of faith, and who is engaged in many different projects throughout America. God has given him the gift to minister to young folks, and I see him using the faith that God has deposited in him.

I thank God for my daughter, Tanya, who has been singing since she was a little girl. As she sings, many of those songs build the faith of the hearers.

I want to acknowledge my eldest son, James DeCuir, who has been such a blessing to me as a prime example of having faith. For years he was in bondage, but we prayed in faith and God set him free. Now he is preaching the unadulterated Gospel of Jesus Christ, and he walks in the faith that God has given him.

One of my other sons, Peter DeCuir, is also preaching the Gospel. I'm grateful for the call of God on his life.

To my son, Rogers DeCuir, Jr., thank you son for your business savvy and for believing in your dad.

To my daughter, Lydia DeCuir, you are the express image of God through all you do in the world of business. Thank you for loving me unconditionally.

I thank God for all of my wonderful children who stood with me in faith down through the years.

I must thank God for all of the members of Holy Deliverance Pentecostal Church who stood with me all of those 50 years. Each one of them took steps of faith with me, and many things happened. We were one of the first black churches in the area that went on television. At one point we were on 17 television stations throughout America, including the Word Network. This all happened because of their faith.

I thank God for Sister Audrey Pichon-Pickens, who worked very hard in helping me prepare this book as well as my first book, *Turn the Page*. She was very helpful in the administration of this book.

Thank God for the publisher of this book who worked tirelessly with me. When she couldn't find me, she called my wife to make sure that I did not give up on this book. Thank you, Dr. Beverly Crockett and the team at Executive Business Writing. I would strongly recommend anyone who has a book project that God has given you to contact her.

I must take time to thank God for my friend, Dr. John Boyd, Sr., who has gone on to heaven, but was such an inspiration to me down through the years. He told me, "Prophet, God gives you revelations. He gives you that rhema word concerning faith, and in other words, you need to put it in print." He was with us when I wrote my first book, and now I know he is rejoicing with me in heaven for writing this second book, *Take the Limits off Your Faith.*

His son, Dr. John Boyd, Jr., has been a great inspiration as well. He told me that God wanted me to come to his church and facilitate a School of Faith. We had it for 5 days. Within that time, we imparted a word of faith to those who attended, that caused their faith to be strengthened. Thank you, Dr. John Boyd, Jr.

I could go on, but without all of these wonderful people, this project would never have been accomplished.

Thank God for you, that as you read this book, you will release your faith. Know this: As you hear the word of faith, your faith is built and your faith is strengthened.

When you have finished reading this book, I want you to have a testimony. You might ask, "What is that testimony, Prophet?" It is this: Your faith is working!

# Introduction

As you release your faith, you must speak words of faith every day. Remember Abraham and Sarah? God promised them a son. Many years went by and there was no son. Sarah was past the years of childbearing, but Abraham kept his faith.

Sarah tried to help God out by letting the maid have a son, but that was not God's plan. The Bible says, *"He staggered not at the promise of God through unbelief; but was strong in faith, giving glory to God; and being fully persuaded that what He had promised, He was able also to perform."* Romans 4:20, 21

You must know that God is going to honor your faith. Declare every day, "I believe God." Faith is a gift from God to all men, "according as God hath dealt to every man the measure of faith." Romans 12:3

Why did God give us a measure of faith? So that we could face challenges, conditions, and circumstances. The measure of faith that you have is powerful.

Remember the scripture: *"If ye have faith as a grain of a mustard seed, ye shall say unto this mountain,*

*Remove hence to yonder place; and it shall remove; and nothing shall be impossible unto you."* Matthew 17:20

Use the measure of faith that God has already given to you. As you use your faith, declare, "My faith is working." Take the limits off your faith. *"Jesus said unto him, if thou canst believe, all things are possible to him that believeth."* Mark 9:23

You cannot allow anything or anyone to move you out of your position of faith. Once you assume the position, don't waver. Don't be up today and down tomorrow.

Every day say, "I believe God; I still believe God, no matter what it looks like." The Bible tells us, *"For therein is the righteousness of God revealed from faith to faith: as it is written, The just shall live by faith."* Romans 1:17

When living by faith, you must take the limits off. Remember, *"Jesus said unto him, if thou canst believe, all things are possible to him that believeth."*

ALL THINGS MEANS ALL THINGS!

# Caveat:

The events described in the following chapters did not necessarily occur in the order in which they are presented.

# Chapter 1
# Miracles and Prayer

My friend, I want you to know that God gave me a prophetic word: Cancellation. Cancellation of every plan of the devil against you—against your body and against your finances. I speak this word over you today, "every plan of the devil against you is canceled. We even cancel his agendas and his attacks against your children. We speak God's protection over their lives no matter where they are. Fear not, for the Lord is on your side. Get ready for a miracle. Believe God. Prayer will fix it."

John 5:1, 2: "*After this there was a feast of the Jews; and Jesus went up to Jerusalem. Now there is at Jerusalem by the sheep market a pool, which is called in the Hebrew tongue Bethesda, having five porches.*" Bethesda means house of mercy. Jesus went up to that pool.

It is a good thing when Jesus shows up in our circumstances. There are things we cannot handle by ourselves. There are some problems we cannot solve; there are some situations we of ourselves cannot turn around. I understand what the Apostle Paul meant when he said, "*I can do all things through Christ that strengthens me."* We need the strength of God to deal with situations; we need the strength of God to go through some of the storms of life; we need the strength of God to survive the attack of the enemy. My friend, you cannot handle it by yourself. Jesus said, *"lo, I am with you always, even unto the end of the world."*

Continuing in John 5:3 and 4, the Bible says, *"In these lay a great multitude of impotent folk, of blind, halt, withered, waiting for the moving of the water. For an angel went down at a certain season into the pool and troubled the water: whosoever then first after the troubling of the water stepped in was made whole of whatsoever disease he had."*

Imagine all of these people waiting but only one could get a miracle. We don't have to wait in line; we don't have to hope that this year maybe I'll get in.

A certain man was there who had his condition for 38 years, watching other people get a miracle. Sometimes we wonder when we see other people delivered from alcoholism, drugs, or spirits, and wish it could happen to us. But it can. God wanted me to remind you that it can happen to you, but you must make yourself available and you must bring your faith to the level at which you know that Jesus can do it for you. He did it for others; He did it for your friends, for your brother, for your mother, for your daddy—why can't He do it for you?

The Bible goes on to say that Jesus approached him, looked at him and knew he had been a long time in that way and He said, *"Wilt thou be made whole?"* John 5:6. In other words, "Are you ready?" You see, He knows how long you have been dealing with the problems, the hurt, the habits, the rejection; how long you have been controlled and manipulated by the spirit of witchcraft, by the spirit of fear, and he wants to know if you want to be made whole? Now, look what the man did. He did what most of us do. We are always trying to find somebody to blame. Who are you blaming?

Here's his response to the Master, *"Sir, I have no man when the water is troubled, to put me into the pool: but while I am coming, another steppeth down before me."* John 5:7. He began to give Jesus his history. How many of us have a bunch of people in the middle of our miracle? Jesus asked him, not the people, "Do you want to be made whole?" and look what the man said, "I don't have anybody to help me."

How many are constantly saying, "I don't have anybody; they abandoned me; they rejected me; they don't like me. Jesus didn't ask him about people, he asked him about him. Many times, we have too many people mixed up in our miracle.

Jesus said, Hold it. Get up and walk. Jesus had heard enough. Sometimes we talk too much. Sometimes we just need to tell God to deliver us from our past. Let your past be what it is. The past. It's already past. We constantly make our past current. We are constantly in the rewind mode. We never let it go. Jesus told the man to get up. You can get up. Just believe God.

# Chapter 2

# I Believe God

Mark 11:22-23: *"And Jesus answering saith unto them, have faith in God. For verily I say unto you, that whosoever shall say unto this mountain, be thou removed, and be thou cast into the sea; and shall not doubt in his heart, but shall believe that those things which he saith shall come to pass; he shall have whatsoever he saith."*

Verse 24 says, *"Therefore I say unto you, what things soever ye desire, when ye pray, believe that ye receive them, and ye shall have them."* Believe that you have it and you have it. Jesus is letting us know that our faith is one of the most powerful gifts that we have. According to the Bible, all of us have faith. The Bible says in Romans 12 that God has given every man a measure of faith. The Word tells us in Mark 11:22, *"And Jesus answering saith unto them have faith in God."*

We must learn to believe God. Why do we have faith in God? Jesus also said in Luke 18:27, *"The things that are impossible with men are possible with God."* Your situation is hard for you, but it is not hard for God.

His word says in Jeremiah 32:27, *"Behold, I am the Lord, the God of all flesh: is there anything too hard for me?"* He is asking you today, Is anything too hard for God – your situation, your marriage, your ministry, that habit? It's not too hard for God.

Nothing is too hard for God. It may be too hard for the doctor, for the lawyer or for the psychiatrist, but it is not too hard for God. I am putting my faith with your faith to decree a miracle in your life. Sometimes the only thing you have left to work with is your faith in God. I believe God for deliverance in every area of your life.

Remember the words that Jesus said in Mark 9:23, *"If thou canst believe, all things are possible to him that believeth."* He is letting you know that when you begin to move in faith, you set yourself up for a miracle. The blind man who was on the roadside begging remembered, it's my time to reposition myself from beggar to believer to receiver. Say, "I believe God. It is my time."

Mark 11:23: *"For verily I say unto you, That whosoever shall say unto this mountain, Be thou removed, and be thou cast into the sea; and shall not doubt in his heart, but shall believe that those things which he saith shall come to pass; he shall have whatsoever he saith."* Do you believe what you say? You have to make your mouth say what your faith is saying. Start saying, "I will live and not die;" start saying what the Word says. "My God shall supply every one of my needs." Start saying, "By His stripes I am healed."

The Bible says that we walk by faith and not by sight. In other words, we look beyond the situation and we see the miracle. If your loved one is on drugs, look beyond the addiction and see them saved and filled with the power of God.

You know different things happen, but you just say, "Oh wow; I believe God." I was ministering in a revival and there was a young woman who was always shouting, but she was always struggling. God told me when I walked down the aisle to say that for somebody in the room, your struggle is over.

Now this young woman had three kids. The whole time she been coming to the meeting she would just shout, but I told her, "You are getting ready to shout up on a miracle." She smiled and I said, "Your struggles are over." And the Lord said, "Challenge her faith." Do you know God will challenge your faith? That night I said to her, "I want you to give the Lord fifty dollars." She said, "Prophet, I don't have fifty dollars." I said, "Well the Lord said give fifty dollars." She said, "I only have five dollars." I told her get in the line. She got in the line and I was going to give her the $50.00, but the Lord said, "Don't give her the fifty dollars."

A young woman was sitting right where she got in the line and reached over and shook her hand and gave her $75.00. I said, "This is the beginning of your miracle."

She had a car full of saints with her that evening, dropping them off in her old beat up car. While she was on her way, a man ran a red light and hit her car. Sabrina and the people in the car start hollering, the blood, the blood of Jesus. You know that used to be a favorite term of the saints. The blood of Jesus. They were in there hollering the blood and this Jewish man got out. He thought they were bleeding because they were saying *the blood.* She was running around the car hollering about the blood and she said, "Oh Lord my insurance isn't right." The man said, "Are you hurt?" She was about to say that she was alright, but she thought about it. One of the saints in the car didn't have the Holy Ghost and they were hollering out "Oh, my back!! My back!!" She was worried about her insurance. This was this man's fourth DUI, so he was saying, "Miss...Please don't call the police," and she was saying, "Please don't call the police because I don't have my insurance right." The man said, "Please ma'am please, please. I beg you, don't call the police." He said, "Meet me tomorrow in Studio City." That's where a whole bunch of rich folks live. "I'm going to get your car straight." He hit a dent that was already dented, but God told her that her struggle was over.

The next day she and the rest of the saints who were in the accident went down there with her. The man said, "This is my brother. He owns this car lot. Go out there and pick whatever car you want, and it's paid for." So, she went out and picked out the car, and they were all praising God. The man said, "My attorney will be here in a minute." She got scared then, and said, "Oh Lord." He said, "I'm going to give you ten thousand dollars, and everybody in the car is going to get five thousand dollars." Then one of the saints said, "I think my knee is hurting" (her back had been hurting at first), and he gave her another $3,000.00. He gave them all money and had them sign a piece of paper that they would not claim any more charges. There was nothing wrong with any of them in any way, but the man was just scared.

God will take advantage of a situation that somebody else is in to bless you. He'll cause somebody to be moved up in their position so you can be in it. He'll create a miracle. Some of you are going to see the greatest shift. New doors are going to open up. Stop worrying about your past. That's already history. The gates of prosperity will never be shut again in your life.

Remember, Jesus admonishes you to say unto the mountain, Be thou removed; be cast into the sea, and not doubt in your heart but believe that those things you say will come to pass. Speak to the mountain. Stop letting the mountains block and stop you. Hurt, failure, pain of divorce, a habit, alcoholism, addiction, perversion, lust—whatever it is—tell God, "Move this mountain out of my life, deliver me today and set me free. I'm tired of being bound; I'm tired of being a prisoner. Loose me." Believe and praise God for your freedom.

# Chapter 3

# The Measure of Faith

Mark 11:22-24: *"And Jesus answering saith unto them, Have faith in God. For verily I say unto you, That whosoever shall say unto this mountain, Be thou removed, and be thou cast into the sea; and shall not doubt in his heart, but shall believe that those things which he saith shall come to pass; he shall have whatsoever he saith. Therefore, I say unto you, what things so ever ye desire, when ye pray, believe that ye receive them, and ye shall have them."*

Many times, we don't feel as though we have faith, but the Bible says that every man, woman, boy, and girl has faith. But what are you doing with your faith? Some people's faith is like a credit card in their pocket, the limit on the credit card is $50,000.00 but they are talking about "I'm hungry; I'm broke," and many times saying faithless things. You have faith but fail to use it. You have got to believe God. He said, *"Whatever you desire, when you pray, believe that you receive them, and you will have them."*

Often, we will hear the prophetic word spoken by the men and women of God, but we don't receive those words. When you receive those words, you will act. On the day that Jesus visited the Pool of Bethesda, there was a man there who "had been an invalid for 38 years" (John 5:5). Jesus asked the man if he wanted to be healed. Jesus said to the man at the pool, "Rise, take up your bed and walk." The man had a choice. He could have said, "Jesus, I can't walk." "I have been here 38 years." But he obeyed, picked up his bed and walked down the street.

When the older generation got through praying, they praised because they knew God was going to do it. They exercised their faith. As a young boy, I remember growing up in Douglasville, Georgia. One day at my grandmother's, we ran out of food. My cousin and I told Big Momma, "We are hungry." She said, "Did you eat all of the tea cakes?" Grandmother made tea cakes regularly for us growing up. "Well," she said, "your grandfather has gone 'coon hunting,' but God will send some food after a while." She then went into the kitchen and started singing an old hymn, 'The Lord Will Make a Way Somehow.' She was boiling water but there was no food. Big Daddy was stuck trying to find a 'coon for the next four days, but her faith spoke to her soul as she declared, "I know the Lord will make a way somehow." Not many moments later, there came a knock on the door, "Mrs. Rachel, is Gordon here?" "No, he isn't," she said. "Well, my wife cleaned out the refrigerator and sent this meat and frozen greens." Big Momma began to praise God and said, "I prayed, and I knew God was going to send food." She expected an answer. Some of you have prayed. Expect an answer – somebody will be delivered; somebody's body will be healed. I speak it today; receive a healing miracle.

Jesus gave us a formula. What you desire when you pray, believe that you will receive it and you shall have it. Don't just pray; believe what you pray. When you pray, expect an answer. Whosoever will say to the mountain, the condition, the situation—get out of my way—get ready for God's favor in your life. Your faith is working.

# The Measure of Faith

# Chapter 4

# Faith for Your Miracle

Matthew 18:19: *"Again I say unto you, That if two of you shall agree on earth as touching anything that they shall ask, it shall be done for them of my Father which is in heaven."*

I am coming into agreement with you right now for a miracle in your life. I don't care what it looks like, I don't care what people are saying, and we are not worried about the prescription. No matter where you are, you are God's child. God has given every man a measure of faith, and I am going to put my measure with your measure. Just step out of the realm of worry and into the realm of faith for your deliverance.

There was a mother who lived in San Bernardino, California. Her son was chosen to preach the gospel when he was a little boy but got caught up on drugs. That mother prayed. Not only did she pray, but she fasted. I implore you, don't stop praying and fasting. I don't care what it looks like or what bad news you hear, your faith is working, and God is going to honor your faith.

This mother fasted over three years and prayed every day. She would come to 12:00 p.m. prayer and let it be known that she was coming specifically for her son to be saved. You must be specific and let God know what you are praying for. Be specific with God.

One Sunday the mother said that she arrived home from church and received a call from her son (her husband answered the phone) who was in prison. He had called from the prison house speaking in tongues and told her he had gotten saved that morning. He told her that his friend convinced him to go to the chapel service and that he didn't want to go.

As the story goes, another young man who had also been to prison now served as a chaplain who had never overseen a chapel service. He was called that Sunday because the regular chaplain and the other chaplains did not show up. God set it up for this woman's son to be delivered. The chaplain gave a portion of his testimony and pointed out her son. He told him to stand up and the chaplain shared his testimony. "I used to be like you. I was chosen to preach but I got caught up on drugs. But my mother never stopped praying." He shared that he had gotten saved and filled with the Holy Ghost after following a girlfriend to church.

The chaplain prayed and in Jesus name commanded that her son be delivered, healed, and saved. The son said the Holy Ghost knocked him out and when he came to himself, he was speaking in tongues. A revival broke out that morning and people were going to the altar crying and weeping. One woman praying for her son caused a whole bunch of sons to get delivered. I admonish you, don't stop praying. Your faith is working. God is going to answer your prayer. Your prayers will be answered.

That woman's son is the pastor of a church now because his mother kept praying the prayer of faith. Do you know how many people have gotten saved because someone was praying? Have you heard that song, 'Somebody Prayed for Me?'

*"And, behold, there came a man named Jairus, and he was a ruler of the synagogue: and he fell down at Jesus' feet, and besought him that he would come into his house."* Luke 8:41

Jairus had a position in church. Many people allow their position to destroy them, to destroy their faith, to destroy their relationship with God because they get caught up in the position and lose their commitment and dedication to God. Sometimes preachers, too, get caught up in their positions.

A preacher told me that he was preaching, he loved God, and he had a good hoop. He said he got caught up in people reacting to his hoop and forgot it wasn't his hoop but the Holy Ghost that does the work. He said, "Before I knew it, I wasn't praying, I wasn't fasting, and I wasn't seeking God for a word, but focusing and concentrating on the hoop. When the enemy came against me, I didn't have any prayer life and it knocked me all the way down. I'm glad it did because it taught me that I can do nothing of myself but all things through Christ."

The Bible tells us that Jairus fell at Jesus' feet and worshipped Him. No matter how gifted you are, you must worship God, you must love God, and not just love your gift. Allow the Holy Ghost to come upon your life and stay humble before God. Allow Him to use you and allow the Holy Spirit to saturate your gift.

Jairus had a need but he worshiped first. His twelve-year-old daughter was dying. You see, Jairus left a dying situation to go and find Jesus. I'm sure people were talking about it. They were probably saying, "How could he leave his family when his daughter was dying?" But Jairus was making a move of faith. After he worshiped Jesus, he made his request for Jesus to come to his house. Jairus had a choice to either stay and watch his daughter die or move out in faith.

He had heard about how Jesus had raised the dead, open blinded eyes, and walked on water, and he believed, "If He can do all that, surely He can heal my daughter."

Jesus was on His way to Jairus' house, but as He went, there were multitudes of people surrounding him. As they crowded Him, a woman with an issue of blood said, "It's my turn." She didn't know where Jesus was going but she knew He was coming her way. Jesus is coming your way. Let Him know what you want and tell Him you need a miracle.

On the way to Jairus' house the woman who had an issue of blood for twelve years got healed. When they got to the house, the Bible says, *"While he yet spake, there cometh one from the ruler of the synagogue's house, saying to him, 'Thy daughter is dead; trouble not the Master.' But when Jesus heard it, he answered him, saying, 'Fear not: believe only, and she shall be made whole.'"* Luke 8:49-50

God is speaking to many of you; your sons and daughters will be delivered. No matter what you hear and no matter what you see, your faith is working. Praise God for the victory and get ready because you haven't seen anything yet!

# Chapter 5

# Take the Limits off Your Faith

A young woman had been praying and believing for a financial miracle. Her house was in foreclosure. She needed $12,000.00. She heard me preaching on the radio about faith. She came to the meeting I was having. I was preaching, "Take the limits off your faith."

All of a sudden, I stopped preaching and told her in seven days she was going to get a miracle from God. She then started shouting (she only had seven days before her house would be sold). I didn't know anything about this woman. I finally asked her, "What are you shouting about?" She told me about her house. She said, "I need a miracle in seven days. I know that my house is coming out of foreclosure."

When I started taking the offering, I asked five people to sow a seed of $100.00. She jumped up and grabbed an envelope and started shouting again. She said, "I know I only have seven days, but I know that this seed I am sowing today shall cause God to release a harvest that shall be enough to pay the bill and bring my house out of foreclosure."

Five days went by and there was no money in sight. But the woman kept on saying that "my faith is working." On the sixth day, she received a call from her brother. He said, "Sis, I won a large sum of money. I am going to deposit a large amount for you to keep so that I don't spend it all. By the way, take, $15,000.00 for yourself." She said she started shouting all over again. She only needed $12,000.00. She took the limit off her faith and she got a miracle.

# Chapter 6

# Believe What You Pray

Matthew 17:20: *"And Jesus said unto them, because of your unbelief: for verily I say unto you, if ye have faith as a grain of mustard seed, ye shall say unto this mountain, remove hence to yonder place, and it shall remove; and nothing shall be impossible unto you."*

There is power in your faith, but you must activate it. Here's how:

1. The words you speak must be in agreement with your faith.

2. You must speak words of faith to realize the power of your faith.

3. Your faith is like the engine in your car. You don't see the engine, but without it, the car will not move. The engine is the power that causes the car to move.

4. Your faith puts you in a position in which things that are impossible become possible.

Remember the scripture, *"And he said, the things which are impossible with men are possible with God."* Luke 18:27

Don't just say words when you pray. Make sure your words are filled with faith. You are talking to God. He is well able to do more than you can ask or think. The words that come out of your mouth after you have finished praying must confirm your faith and the prayer that you prayed. If you prayed for your husband to be saved, start saying, "My husband is going to be saved."

There was a young woman whose husband was not saved. He spent more time at his girlfriend's house than he did at his own home. His wife was very depressed and thinking about dying. She came into one of the faith clinics I had one afternoon in Atlanta, Georgia. In that session, I said to the people, "Pray the prayer of faith concerning your loved ones."

What is the prayer of faith? It is knowing that God is going to do it. After the prayer of faith, don't be afraid to say that God is going to do it. After this young lady prayed, it looked like her husband had gotten worse, but she kept saying, "My husband is going to be saved."

She stopped fussing with him and released her faith. One day he came home and told her he was going out of town for the weekend, but it was a lie; he was actually going out of town with his girlfriend to her brother's funeral.

He and his girlfriend were sitting in the funeral service. While the preacher was preaching, the power of

God began to fall, and people started praising God. The man of God who preached was a prophet. As he looked out at the people in the service, he stopped preaching and called out the husband who was with the young woman who was unsaved and started ministering to him. He laid his hand on him and he fell out under the power of God.

While he was out under the power of God, the preacher prayed for the girlfriend. God knocked her out under the power. The girlfriend was a backslider and she got restored at the funeral service. The husband got saved and filled with the Holy Ghost at the funeral service.

The wife got a phone call from her husband who was speaking in tongues. He repented, as did the girlfriend who sent him home to his wife. Look what happened when the wife changed her position of fussing, prayed the prayer of faith, and began speaking the words of faith; she experienced a miracle from God.

Believe What You Pray

# Chapter 7

# Unusual Miracles

1 Corinthians 15:58: *"... be ye steadfast, unmovable, always abounding in the work of the Lord ..."*

I have a friend who lives in Detroit. He wanted a certain house, but there was no way that he could get it. Neither the owner nor his wife wanted to sell their home. So, my friend's wife went to the house, anointed it with oil, laid hands on it, and prayed the prayer of faith in the front yard.

The owners of the house kept saying that they didn't want to sell the house. It wasn't what they were saying but it is what God says. The man's wife's faith was working.

A year went by and the husband said to his wife, "I'm tired of hearing about that house. They don't want to sell the house." She went to church and the preacher asked someone to sow a seed offering of $2,000.00. She looked at her husband and he looked everywhere but at her. Before he knew it, his wife was in the offering line giving the $2,000.00. He said, "Lord help my wife." She took off running around the church and did about three or four laps. (God will give you the confirmation that your faith is working.)

The husband was upset with his wife but he didn't say anything to her at that moment. Three weeks later the realtor called and said the family wanted to set up a meeting with my friend and his wife. (God will set up a meeting with you and your miracle.) The husband later told his wife, "the people want to sell the house."

My friend's wife kept saying that she was going to get her house. When they arrived, the owner said, "I understand that you want to buy our house." He proceeded to inform them that his wife had been diagnosed with cancer and they had made the decision to move to Switzerland in order to be closer to their daughter. He wanted to know if they were still interested in buying the house. He said to them, "You seemed like you were so sincere."

The wife said, "Please sir, excuse me for a minute. I have to go and give God praise right now." She put some praise with her faith. The owner told them whatever he had to do to help them get the house, he would be willing to do. He stated if he had to knock $50,000.00 off the price, he would. God will make people do whatever they have to do to get your miracle to you.

# Chapter 8

# My Husband Is on the Way

Mark 11:24: *"Therefore I say unto you, what things soever ye desire, when ye pray, believe that ye receive them, and ye shall have them."*

A woman who had heard me tell this story for five years got married last year. I told her to start seeing herself in the kitchen cooking. She said to me, "Prophet Decuir, I did what you told me to do and it doesn't seem like anything is happening." Her little girl had heard the prophecy and said to her, "Mommy, the prophet said my daddy is coming and I sure wish he would hurry up."

I've told the story about a woman who had come to one of my meetings. I told her to give $100.00 and it was her last $100.00. (While you are giving, God is adding more to your faith account). I told her to go home and set a place at the table for her husband. She started shouting and praising God because I told her that she was going to get married. I said, "When you get home, get a plate, knife, fork, and a napkin." She asked where she was to put it and I told her to put it on the table in the kitchen. She was obedient to the word that was given.

She had three little girls and one of them asked, Momma, who is that plate for?" She told them the plate was for their dad. They began to make fun of her asking where he is, "We don't see him," and she would say, "He's sitting right there."

So, the oldest girl asked her mom where she had been that day, that she would sit at the table and talk to a plate. She told her that she had gone to the 12:00 p.m. service with me and that I had told her God was going to send her a husband. Her daughter said, "Momma, you are sitting here talking to this plate, but I bet Prophet Decuir is not sitting somewhere talking to a plate."

For two months the lady came to the 12:00 p.m. service and I continued to tell her that her husband was coming. Daily, her children would talk to the plate and when they would finish eating, they would say, "Alright Daddy, we're going upstairs to do our homework and then go to bed. Goodnight."

One day the woman heard about a stocking sale at Macy's and decided to go to the store to make a purchase. While she was in the store, it began to pour down rain. When she got into her car, it wouldn't start. (Note: Some storms are good for you, and some storms will set you up). The lady didn't know anything about fixing cars so she was under the hood saying, "Satan, the Lord rebuke you in the name of Jesus." Along came a man in a truck and asked her what was wrong with the car. She looked and him and said, "Do I look like I know?"

He told her that he was a mechanic and got out of the truck to see what he could do, but at the time he couldn't fix it. It wasn't God's timing. He asked her if he could give her a ride home and she accepted. While in the truck she fussed with him the whole time about old chicken bones everywhere in his truck. He told her that she was the one who needed a ride. While they were riding along, a hole developed in the roof of the truck on his side. He began to get wet while she stayed dry. (God was setting it up.)

When they got to her house, she asked him if he wanted to come in to dry off, and he said, "Yes, that would be nice." When he went in, he sat in the chair where the plate was set up. The girls were upstairs and the little girl told her sisters there was a man downstairs that they had never seen before. So, all three girls started down the stairs and started peeping. All of a sudden, the little girl's faith became alive and she ran downstairs and said, Momma, Momma, Momma! God has sent us a daddy and he's sitting in the chair!"

The man asked what it meant and she told him that she had three little girls and that they were all silly and not to pay any attention to them. So, their mother made them go back upstairs, but the little girls spoke words that had already begun to come to fruition.

The man came back the next day and the car still would not start. He offered to take her to Sunday evening church service. He had been a backslider for over 14 years and that night, he was born again.

On that Monday morning, he came back and picked her up. He began to tell her that the Lord had told him that she was his wife. She asked, "What are you talking about, we just met on Saturday." He said the Lord had told him when he drove up to help fix her car that she was his wife. When they got to her car, it started up. They got married that same day.

When they picked the children up from school, they took them out to eat and he told them that she was his new wife and they were going to their new house and for them not to take anything from the old house but clothes. He gave her two brand new credit cards and told them that the next day, they would go and buy everything new.

They went to his house and it had everything the girls wanted inside. They each had their own room and she had a St. Charles kitchen inside, just waiting for her. She found out that he owned five demolition yards and 14 rental properties in Dallas, Texas.

He was a millionaire and she became a millionaire the moment she signed the marriage certificate and didn't even know it. In the garage, he had a brand-new already paid for Mercedes Benz waiting for her.

My Husband Is on the Way

# Chapter 9

# Strong Faith That Works

Luke 18:27: *"But He said, The things which are impossible with men are possible for God." (NKJV)*

There was a lady who received a call that her daughter had died in an accident. The prophet was asked to call her and tell her about her daughter. When he started talking to her, she immediately began to say, "My daughter is not dead."

She had two older sons and they were beside themselves with grief over their sister. Another member called the prophet and said, "She is in shock. I called the highway patrol again and they confirmed that the daughter was dead."

The highway patrol said there were some girls in an accident on the road back from Las Vegas, headed to Los Angeles and one of the girls in the car was dead. I called this sister back and told her that I had spoken to the highway patrolman and he told me that her daughter was dead. In a condescending tone she said to me, "Pastor, I don't mean to be disrespectful towards you, but my daughter is not dead."

One of the members of the church suggested that we take her to the hospital and have her checked out and that she probably needed to be put on some type of medication. Another member of the church who had access to all the details and was receiving frequent updates told us that she had indeed passed away. This sister spoke once again and said, "Pastor, I haven't shed one tear. God said my daughter is not dead."

I asked the gentleman at the hospital to call everyone that he could to make sure and 45 minutes later he called us back and said, "Reverend, you're not going to believe this but there were two car accidents. One girl they flew to Las Vegas and the other to Banning and the one whom they flew to Banning is this lady's daughter. She's in a coma and they don't think she is going to live, but she's alive right now."

I called her back and told her that her daughter was not dead, but they were saying that she was in critical condition and it looked like she wasn't going to survive. This sister kept her faith and continued to repeat, "She is not dead, nor will she die." She went to the hospital and confidently repeated what she said that day.

Her daughter stayed in a coma for 15 days and did not move. For a while, a lot of people were quick to lose faith because of the circumstances, but that young lady had the right mother, who continued to pray and use her faith. I want you to know that after that 15th day, the girl got up. It has now been three years since that happened. I dare you to start saying what God is going to do and don't take it back.

# Chapter 10

# Make Your Mouth Say What Your Faith Is Saying

Proverbs 3:5,6: *"Trust in the LORD with all thine heart; and lean not unto thine own understanding. In all thy ways acknowledge him, and he shall direct thy paths."*

I was a young man and I didn't know anything about this faith stuff, but I knew Jesus. I had been preaching to ducks and chickens since I was a kid.

One night I heard this guy on the radio preaching and I said, "I'm going to that meeting." My son, Rogers Jr., had just been born and his momma told me to bring back some milk for our son and some eggs and bacon. I had $4.00 in my pocket. I decided to stop and hear the man's sermon. There were quite a lot of people there that night and out of all the people he turned and said to me, "Young man, the Lord wants you to give everything in your pocket." Right away I said, "Oh no. I can't do that. I've got to bring Jr. some milk." So, the service went on and he must have raised an offering of about $2,000.00.

As he prepared to leave, he put on his coat and said to me, "Son, did you give everything in your pocket?" I said,

"No sir." I started to say that I had to get my baby some milk, when he interrupted by saying, "Obey God. God said to give it and watch him cause a miracle that will happen within the next 24 hours." Reluctantly, I gave it because it wasn't a joy to give it, knowing that my boy's momma was going to ask about the milk.

Driving home, I remembered singing the words to the song, *'I know the Lord will make a way, I know He will.'* After singing that song, I started praying, "Put Junior to sleep, Lord."

When I got back home, I eased in the door and sure enough Junior was sleeping and so was his mother. Relieved, I slid into the bed, but five minutes later Junior began to cry. I was saying, "Satan, the Lord rebukes you." Then Junior began to cry louder. His mother said, "Why can't you just give him some milk?" I told her to give him to me. I put him on me and started singing. He continued to holler so much that his mother got up and said, "Where is the milk?" I told her that he was going to be alright. Then she turned on the lights and said, "Please tell me that you didn't give the preacher my baby's milk money." I told her that I had to obey God, and that I felt it in my spirit.

I kept telling the baby to be quiet and not to let the devil use him. When I said that he sure enough hollered. I finally remembered the trick of putting some sugar on a cloth and dipping it in water. He began to sip it and finally went back to sleep. I still had the task to find milk for the baby to drink in the morning.

About 4 o'clock in the morning, someone started knocking very hard on the door. I asked my wife to get the door, but she insisted that I be the one to open it. I asked her once more, and she ended up being the one to go check to see who was at the door. Not even two minutes of her being downstairs, she started hollering. A woman who had also been at the revival that I attended started jumping up and down and speaking in tongues. I asked, "What's going on?" My wife beckoned to me, "Come here, come here." The lady had backed her station wagon up to the front door. She said that she was in her bed asleep and the Lord woke her up and told her to go buy Little Brother Rogers and his family some groceries. The first thing she brought out of the car was a case of Similac™ milk (which contained 24 cans)! (Remember, the preacher said within 24 hours).

If I had kept the $4.00, it would have only been enough money to purchase one can of milk. In addition, she had steaks, pork chops, and much, much more food. I had to take that step of faith. I learned early on, if you move in faith, God will move with a miracle for you.

Make Your Mouth Say What Your Faith is Saying

# Chapter 11

# Move on Someone Else's Faith

Mark 9:23: *"... If thou canst believe, all things are possible to him that believeth."*

I was in Mississippi conducting a revival, and it was looking financially slim. I called the pastor and talked to him about it and he said to challenge the faith of those in attendance. He shared with me that God was going to meet the financial need.

It was raining that night and I asked the pastor for 100 envelopes. I shared with the congregation that God wanted them to bring an offering in the amount of $80.00 on the upcoming Friday night. One lady said, "How much?" She said that she only made $123.00.

There was an older woman who rose from her seat to take an envelope and told me that she had no money at all and only received social security, but she was going to bring her $80.00 at the appointed time. I asked those in attendance to start saying what the seasoned mother had said. Every night when that mother came, she would leap with joy and repeatedly said that she was going to have her money on Friday. People in the congregation started taking envelopes and declaring they too would have the requested offering on Friday.

The closer it got to Friday however, Mother started losing her faith. She told me that she didn't have the money and I reminded her that Friday hadn't arrived yet. By 12:00 p.m. on Friday, she came in the door of the church, running very quickly. I asked her what the matter was and she said, "God gave me a miracle." Her brother had come over and wanted her to cook him some breakfast. Reluctantly, she prepared fish and grits for her brother's breakfast.

Suddenly, her brother started crying and told her, "Lillie, Lillie, Lillie! I have done you wrong." She said, "No you haven't done anything wrong to me." He told her, "Yes, I did. I was listening to the preacher on television and he said if we don't get some things right, we are going to die and go to hell. Lillie, I don't want to roast like a pig and bake like a peanut, and in hell lift up my eyes." She said, "Bob, what did you do?" He asked her to forgive him and took an envelope out of his pocket and threw it on her kitchen table. The envelope was full of money. She said, "Where did you steal all this money from?" He said, "Lillie, I didn't steal it. When Daddy died, he told me to divide the money with everybody. Instead, I kept it all for myself, but I had to give it to you today."

My God! Mother started shouting and praising God and declaring, "I have never had $39,000.00 in my whole life!" She gave her tithes and an offering of $1,000.00 that night. My faith wasn't working, but I took the word of the pastor, and God performed a miracle.

Move on Someone Else's Faith

# Chapter 12
# It's Canceled – Right Now

Ephesians 6:10-12: *"Finally, my brethren, be strong in the Lord and in the power of His might. Put on the whole armor of God, that you may be able to stand against the wiles of the devil. For we do not wrestle against flesh and blood, but against principalities, against powers, against the rulers of the darkness of this age, against spiritual hosts of wickedness in the heavenly places."* (NKJV)

There was a lady at one of my revivals in Detroit and we were speaking cancellation of every plan of the devil. She was going around the church speaking, "It's canceled, it is canceled, in the name of Jesus." She did not know that she was canceling the plan that the devil had to murder her son that night.

There is power in the word. When she got home, she realized that her son was at home. She said to herself, what is going on; Junior said he was going out. She looked in the room and he was in the bed asleep. Her son had called her and told her that he was going out, but when he went outside to leave, all four of his tires had been flattened. So, he got angry and said that he was just going to go to bed.

Later that night around 1:30 a.m., the phone rang. Her son's friend was on the phone crying, saying four of his friends got killed that night, and her son was supposed to be with them.

When she told her son about how she had prayed in the church that night and spoke cancellation of any plan of the devil against him, he went to church the next night and got saved. You'd be surprised by what a word will do. God honored that mother's prayer and her faith.

A pastor once said to me, "Prophet, just tell the Lord to speak to you." He always wanted the word to come directly from God. So, when my plane was three or four hours late, I just said, "Lord, I'm going to use this time to pray." One of the things I want you to do (and there's a word God gave me just before this year came in), He said we must begin to cancel the activity of the devil. We have to begin to speak words of cancellation. So, whatever the enemy has planned against you is canceled.

You know, even the secret things—even the things the devil thinks we don't know about—they are canceled. Not one plan, but every plan. I want you to know that every plan that the devil is trying to work against you, I cancel it in the name of Jesus. I cancel it. Whatever it is.

You don't know what the devil is working against your son, but it's canceled. Canceled! It will not come to pass. It will not do what he thinks it's going to do. It's already canceled, in the name of Jesus.

For your son, for your daughter—oh, it's already canceled. It doesn't matter where they are or what they're doing. Every plan, known and unknown, is canceled right now. Accidents are canceled. Murders are canceled. Come on. It's already canceled.

When I was on the plane, the pilot told us something was wrong, but they never told us what was wrong. Have you ever noticed the airport folks will tell you something is wrong, but they never tell you what it is? I didn't see any mechanics, so I knew there was nothing wrong with the aircraft. We were supposed to leave at 9:05 pm. They came at 10:00 pm and said, "We'll be departing after a while." Well, after a while could be in the morning.

So finally, I said, "Lord, I speak Your word. And the word says...no weapon formed against you shall prosper. And I started speaking that word. Finally, the man said, "We aren't leaving until around 1:00 am in the morning. I had been at the airport since 8:00 pm, but God had it all under control.

God has everything under control. I don't care what it looks like. I don't care what that doctor said. God's got it all under control. Don't you care what your haters are saying...that doesn't even matter. I don't care what the banker said. God's got it all under control. All of it.

Now, you know the enemy is on the warpath and all, but it isn't working. Because it looked like the plane wasn't going anywhere, I was wondering, when the plane gets to the destination, is it going to be able to go back? But the Lord said, "Speak the word." Whatever the enemy has planned is canceled.

Whatever warfare you've been in, you've already survived it. The devil didn't even believe you'd be reading this, and he thought he had worn out your praise. But somebody who's been in the war can say, "I've yet got a praise. I might have been wounded but I've yet got a praise. I might have gotten a little discouraged, but I've yet got a praise."

And see...you don't realize that when you go through things, if it doesn't do anything but bring a greater bonding between you and God, you didn't go through that in vain. You're closer to God now and you know more about God. Glory to God. So, we've all got to learn that going through isn't so bad after all. And that's why the Word says all things work together for your good.

Now the Word didn't say all things are good, but it did say that they are going to work together. See, when you go through and come out mad and bitter, it didn't work for your good. But when you go through and come out with a praise...it worked for your good. When you come out saying, "Glory!" When you come out saying, "Hallelujah!" When you come out saying, "I'm going to bless Him anyhow. I'm going to praise Him anyhow," that means it worked together for your good.

You see, we're in an hour now...we're in a season in which the devil wants all of us to be discouraged by our past. Your past has already passed. God's doing something new for you right now.

You're dealing with some old stuff and it's new...NEW! It's a new season...it's a new time. You know, some people will never go anyplace because they live on Past Street. You have to move over to Future Street. You have to move over into the now. God's blessing you right now and you are going to have what God says you're going to have and you're going to be what God says you're going to be! And it doesn't matter what anyone else says.

There was a little girl about three or four years old who heard me preach about faith—what God will do. I said, if you believe God, you can have what you want. And she was just jumping and we couldn't stop her from jumping. And so, her momma said, "Sit down," and she wouldn't sit down. So, after church she came and she said, "Prophet?" I said, 'Yes." "You said if I believed God, I could have what I want." I said, "That's right." And she danced a little more. But I didn't know why she was doing it. So finally, she said, "Prophet?" I said, "Yes?" She said, "I want fifty dollars." I said, "what are you going to do with fifty dollars?" She said, "I want this doll." She named some doll. "My momma can't buy it, but you said I could have what I want," and she went to dancing. And I just reached in my pocket (I happened to have it) and I gave her $50.00, and I said, "Here." She ran back hollering all down the hall, "Prophet gave me $50.00! He said I could have what I want!"

See, some of you have to realize you're in that season. You're in that season where everything God said about you is getting ready to happen, but you have to have enough faith to remind God of what He said about you. And, see what happened was after that, every Sunday...her momma would tell her, "Sit down!" She'd sit down for a minute then run back up there. She said, "Prophet?" I said, "Yes." She said, "that was such a good message and I can have what I say." I said, "What are you going to say?" "I just want some ice cream this time."

This little girl had big faith. At that time, we had about 15 children, and she would say to them, "Tell Prophet..." She had programmed them, that all you have to do is ask. All you have to do is say what God has already said, and He's going to do it.

Why don't you say what God has already said? Why don't you say it? Why don't you say, "God's going to heal me?" Why don't you say, "I am blessed?" Why don't you say, "The devil is a lie!" Why don't you say, "I'm coming out!" Why don't you say, "I'm coming through!" Why don't you say it?

All you have to do is use your mouth. Do you know your mouth is one of the greatest means of victory? Why don't you use your mouth...to say what you know God's going to do?

See now that little girl, she's growing up. Her momma said every time she wants something from her, she says, "Momma, God said I could have what I want." Her momma didn't have a husband, but the little girl started telling momma, "Momma, God's going to send you a husband and that's going to be my daddy and he's going to be rich." She said she'd just tell the little girl, "I hope he is." And she said every now and then she would just say it. She said she kept on saying it until she would start embarrassing her. She started telling folk, "God's going to send me a daddy. He's going to be my momma's husband and he's going to be rich."

I dare you to start saying what God's going to do. You're in that season. Stop talking about what you've been through. You've already been through it. Start saying, "I'm going to have what God says I'm going to have." Start saying, "My children are going to be saved."

The mother of this child went to visit a big church that thousands of folks attended. She said of the church, "You know...it was alright." She said that she just went because her sister goes there. God's already got a setup, so all you have to do is show up. God already knows what you need.

There are so many people that attend this church, they have two or three parking lots. It's just so congested over there, even just to park. If you really didn't want to go there, you'd go home because the parking is a test. But she said she had to walk about three blocks and went in and attended the service.

When she came out, the front tire on her car was flat. She was sitting there going through all kinds of changes. "Lord, my tire's flat." Her automobile club card had expired. She didn't have enough money to pay for a tow, and all of a sudden, a man drove up in a beautiful Lexus, rolled down the window and said, "Is something wrong?" She said, "my tire is flat." He said, "Well, we're going to take care of that." And he got out and said, "We've got to call the automobile club because you don't even have a spare tire." Listen...God's already got it prearranged.

Some of you are going to get some prearranged miracles. Prearranged. That means it's already set up.

The man called the automobile club and they came out and fixed her tire. He told her, "Follow me to the gas station." He filled her car up with gas. And the little girl was in the car saying, "Mommy…" She told her, "Shut up! Don't you say it!"

God is trying to speak to you and you don't want to hear it. Open your ears so you can hear. God's trying to tell somebody, tonight is your time. You're in a season in which God is getting ready to manifest what you've been praying for, for three years, for five years. Throw your hands up and tell Him, "Thank You!"

God is saying, "Unusual favor." And He's saying, "It's getting ready to manifest. And it's going to look to some folks like it came out of nowhere." But this came from the heart of God. Now the enemy's going to know you're blessed. Your haters are going to know you're blessed. If you have some haters, they're going to watch you in a season of FAVOR."

The man filled her car up with gas and asked the gas station attendant, "Can they park their car here?" "I'm taking them to dinner." She said, "Hold it!" And the little girl said, "Momma?" She had to hit her… "Hush!" The little girl was about to confirm…Ooh…Glory to God! This is a confirmation for you right now because God's getting ready to manifest everything that He ever said concerning you. EVERYTHING!

God's got a record of everything that He ever said about you. God's got a record of every prayer you ever prayed. God's got a record of every prophesy that's ever been spoken over your life. God's got a record of every shut-in that you've ever gone on. God's got a record of every fast and God sent a prophet by to tell you He's getting ready to manifest. Every wall has got to fall. Every stumbling block has got to move. Every door that's locked up has to open up. It's getting ready to manifest. It's going to manifest. Everything!

Somebody's going to know after a while. Everybody's going to know that the Lord is on your side. Everybody's going to know that you're in a season of manifestation. The next seven months, favor, favor, favor. Double favor. Special favor. Look out. You're going to be overwhelmed with miracles.

It's already set up. You can start shouting already. God's getting ready to make up for everything you went through in the last five years. God's getting ready to make up for everything you've ever gone through. He's going to renew your joy. He's going to renew your strength. Your faith is going to a whole other level. You're going to see miracles in every area of your life. Every area!

The man told her, "I'm taking you and your daughter to dinner." She said she wanted to tell him she didn't want to go and she said the little girl said, "Momma, I'm hungry." See, sometimes God has to use somebody to help you out. That's why when you go to church you have to have somebody to speak a word to help you out. God is getting ready to manifest everything that you prayed about. I hear Habakkuk say, *"though it tarried..."* It might have been held up. It might have been delayed. But I prophesy the delay is over. I prophesy the hold back is over. I prophesy the setback is over. I prophesy the warfare is over. I prophesy breakthrough. I prophesy breakout. Lift your hands and say, "Yes!"

The man took her and the little girl to dinner and the little girl asked...you know God was using that little girl— she asked, "What kind of work do you do?" And the man said, "I'm an attorney." And she said, "Are you one of those lawyers? Our teacher was teaching us about Brother Johnnie Cochran..." And he said, "Yes." He said, "Johnnie's gone to heaven." She said, "You're still here..." And I want you to know that the rest is history. The mother is his wife now. And the little girl tells everybody, "I told you God was going to send my momma a husband and he's going to be rich." You have to start saying what you know God's going to do. Don't be afraid to say, "It's my time." Don't be afraid to say, "I'm coming out." Don't be afraid to say, "I'm stepping over it." Don't be afraid to say, "I'm going through it."

Now the Word says in Mark 11:22, *"Whosoever shall say to the mountain.... whosoever."* If you have enough faith to say it, God's got enough power to do it. And you have to throw it in the devil's face. It's going to happen.

Now, you're in a season in which what your enemy says doesn't even matter. And the credit bureaus can't hold you back. A woman who lives in Detroit said her credit rating wasn't even on the bureau's scale, but she came to the meeting and I said, "Girl,"—God just gave it to me...I didn't know what she was going to say—"you want a Lexus, that little utility....that pretty little utility vehicle." She said, "I sure do." She said, "I can't have it though." I said, "Why can't you have it?" She said, "I was married...I lost everything—my house, my car..." And she said, "My husband just messed my credit up." I said, "but the Lord said to go and get it."

You just have to go get some stuff. Stop letting the devil tell you what you can't have. And I said, "I want you to believe God and start saying I'm going to have that Lexus utility truck." And she started saying it.

I was in Detroit for 10 days that time and every night she would give $50.00, or $20.00. And one time I felt bad, you know, but I had to do it because God said, "Girl, empty your purse out. Give everything." I didn't know it was snowing and she said, "I don't have a way to get home." I said, "Somebody give her a ride." And I said, "Here." But then I said, "No. The Lord told me I can't help you." And so, a preacher gave her a $100.00 on the way home. She didn't even know if he had a wife or not. And I want you to know she kept saying it and every night she said, "I'm going to have..." Learn to keep saying what you know God's going to do. Keep saying it. Everything is going to be better.

I told someone in the audience to touch the lady in front of her and tell her, "God just told the prophet to tell you everything's going to be better." Everything.

You know what God does? He goes back, and that's what God's doing for the saints now. He's going back and making up for everything that they went through in past years. Restoration and their heart's desire are what they are getting ready to experience.

You have to know what season it is. One year I was in a great financial battle, and a bishop laid hands on me and said, "Prophet, receive the greatest financial overflow you've ever had." I caught that word. Everybody started giving to me...even people who didn't like me. Similarly, you're getting' ready to have a season of restoration, and God's going to use everybody. Everybody's going to bless you. Every time you go to the mailbox, be looking for miracles.

The lady who wanted the Lexus went down to the Lexus place and told the salesman, "I want a new utility truck off the floor." She said, "I don't want a used one." Make it known to God what you want and start saying what He's going to give you. She told him what the Word said: "*Whosoever shall say to the mountain be thou removed; be thou cast into the sea and shall not doubt in his heart but shall believe that those things ... he shall have whatsoever he says.*" And the salesman said, "You must be a Christian." She said, "I'm saved...you know—sanctified, filled with the Holy Ghost." He said, "My momma is, too." And she said, "You ain't nothing but an old backslidden preacher." He asked her, "What are you talking about?" She said, "You're just a preacher." She started, "When you were a little boy..." He started weeping like a baby.

It's already settled. All you have to do is show up. God's going to do something miraculous.

She started praying and the salesman got reclaimed. They were praising God and he was speaking in tongues. Then she said, "I want my Lexus. I'm driving it home." With all kinds of bad credit, she said, "I'm driving it home."

Start saying what God's going to do. The salesman said, "Sis, there's no way you can have this new Lexus. I might be able to get you in a used one." She said, "I don't want a used Lexus. I know what I want."

Don't you know what you want? The salesman called the manager, who was one of the owners. He said, "She wants this car. I just gave my heart back to God." The manager said, "Well, give me her application. I'm going to co-sign. I'm the owner." She began shouting and drove off in a brand-new Lexus.

God's already got it set up. He's got the way already made, but you have to start saying it. Why don't you say what God's going to do; say it about your children. Say it about your son. Say it about your daughter. Say it about your body. Lay hands on your own self and say, "I'm healed in the name of Jesus."

Now we are in a season in which God is going to manifest what He's already said, but we've got to let our faith connect to what He's already said. See, a lot of people hear it, but they don't let their faith connect and they don't start saying what they know God's going to do.

In this season of favor, you're going to see God move in every area of your life. Some things are going to turn around. Your loved ones are going to turn around. I don't care what they're doing; God's going to honor your faith. I don't care what they said this morning; God's going to honor your faith. I don't care what the bank said; God's going to honor your faith. God's going to touch people in high places. He's going to give you favor.

God said, "It's your season." And in this season of favor, He's going to manifest what your haters thought wasn't going to be manifest.

I'm rejoicing with you even now because of what God is getting ready to do. Rejoicing because of the divine reversal of everything that the devil thought he had accomplished. Rejoicing because of the manifestation. Rejoicing because of favor in high places. Shout, "Everywhere I go I'm going to have favor."

Favor! You are going to have favor if you go to the courthouse. If you go down to the bank. If you go over to your children's house. Don't you worry; you're walking in favor. You are going to have what God said you'll have. Don't you worry; you've already survived the worst. You've already come through what you thought you weren't coming through. And now you're walking in favor. Nothing will set you back. Nothing will hold you down. You are walking in favor.

Favor! You know when you fool with folks who have favor, you're crazy. Pharaoh thought he was going to kill Baby Moses. Moses was a baby, but he had favor. The devil thought the fire was going to burn up Shadrach, Meshach, and Abednego, but it couldn't burn them up. Why? Because they had favor. Joseph's brothers said, "We're going to finish him off." Eleven brothers against one, but Joseph had favor.

It doesn't matter what the doctors say you're dealing with. You've got favor from the Chief Surgeon. No weapon formed against you shall prosper because you have favor. A 1,000 shall fall at your side, 10,000 at your right hand, but it's not going to come nigh you because you have favor. No plague is coming near your house because you have favor. The accident the devil had set up will never come to pass because you have favor. Lift your hands and say thank you for favor!

That is why God has you in a season of cancellation—because of favor. Remember that scripture, that if you don't doubt in your heart, but believe that those things that you say shall come to pass, you shall have what you say.

# Chapter 13

# I'm in a Season of Great Manifestation

Note from the publisher: This is an excerpt from a message from 2016 that is relevant and can be applied to your life today.

In June 2015, I started wondering what was going on. And then in August I started wondering when December 31st was coming. But it looked like something happened. There was a shift in the realm of the Holy Ghost. In September I wasn't worried about it. Now I can say, "I survived 2015."

Your enemy didn't think you would, but you survived it. Your haters didn't think you would, but you survived it. Hallelujah! And you yet have a praise. You have the victory.

One of the things that 2015 taught you—it taught you how to take a punch and then another punch. And then some of you took another punch. But it didn't knock you out. You took the punch, but every time, you bounced back with a praise. And people don't realize what fasting and prayer does. It sets you up for every challenge that the devil is going to bring. The devil is a fool because we're fasting this year, and none of his punches last year knocked us out, and none of them are going to knock us out this year. We have learned how to survive under the pressure. We've learned how to take the punch. We've learned how to bounce back with a praise. And 2015 taught some people how to be committed to God. That year caused many of us to make a new commitment.

It also made many of us realize that God wants dedication. The more you pray, the more you become dedicated. And then if you keep on praying, you become consecrated. So, one thing that 2015 did was cause the prayer life of many believers to intensify.

There's something about when you get punched on: it hurts, but it conditions you. Last year was a year of conditioning and preparing you for what God's got set up. Sometimes those punches were coming from places you did not expect, but all of a sudden, the devil hit you. You tried to recover from that and then he hit you again. But because of the power you had, he could not knock you out. You survived it. There's nothing like a survivor. A survivor has a testimony. A survivor has a greater relationship with God. I don't know about you, but I'm ready for 2016. It is the year that God is going to open every gate that the devil thought he had shut.

The year 2016 is the year that God is going to release double power. Double anointing. And 2016 is the year of restoration. The year of release. It's the year of recovery. There's going to be such an outpour in the church. There's a fresh oil anointing. That anointing that not only makes you dance but will break every yoke off your life. It's an anointing that will move every mountain. It's an anointing that will break every stronghold. This is the year you've been waiting on.

This new year is also the year of crossing over. You know, nobody had more prophesies than the Israelites on their life. And even though they were going through, they had some word on their life. Joshua 1:1: *"Now after the death of Moses, the servant of the Lord, it came to pass that the Lord spoke to Joshua, the son of Nun..."*

*After.* All you have to do is wait until the thing is over. God's going to always move *after.* When the devil thinks it's going to kill you, God always moves on your behalf. I believe there's somebody whom the enemy did not expect to be here in 2016, but you're here.

The Bible says that perhaps the most devastating thing that ever happened in their lives was the death of Moses. I'm sure they thought, how is God going to talk to us; what are we going to do? Oh, but God. God's already got it set up. It's beyond your imagination.

*The servant of the Lord.* Now the Bible describes Moses as the servant. A servant. I wonder how many people don't mind being a servant. The old folks used to have a song they'd sing, 'Any way you use me.'

Now the Bible says that after the death of Moses, God spoke to Joshua, the son of Nun, Moses' minister, saying, *Moses my servant is dead.* (v. 2) The year 2015 is over. You've already survived it but get ready for manifestation.

The Lord said that 2016 is the year of great manifestation. God had already told me, and so this year 2016 is a year of believers, if you can connect your faith to it. See, God can send a word, but a word is only a word that will hang over your head if you don't connect your faith to it. Manifestation!

Now the Bible says, after the death of Moses, the Lord spoke unto Joshua, the son of Nun, Moses' minister saying, Moses my servant is dead. In other words, that period right there is over. God's getting ready to do something new in your life. He's going to move everything out of your way. God's getting ready to manifest, but there's some stuff you have to move. There's some stuff you have to cross over. Whatever's been in your way, move it out of your way because you have to have that manifestation. You have to have what God said. You have to let the plan of God be done in your life.

You see, all of these prophetic words come and sometimes when they don't manifest, we say, well, that preacher or that woman was not telling the truth. But a lot of times you have to step over some stuff for that word to manifest.

God told Elijah to go down to the brook Cherith, and He said, *"When you get there, I'm going to command the ravens to feed you there."* Just get to that right place and you are going to see nothing but manifestation.

So now the Bible says Joshua spake unto them. Verse 2: *"...Now, therefore arise..."* Now He gave him an order. They'd been in this wilderness all these years, wandering. Moses had just died, they're depressed, and they're grieved. Have you ever noticed you learn better under pressure? You learn better and God works better. God will always prove to you that He's God. That's why you never have all the answers, but God's already got it figured out. All you have to do is show up. He said, *"Arise and go over this Jordan..."* (verse 2)

Now God gave them an order. Go over that Jordan. He didn't tell them how they were going to get over it. They didn't have a boat...didn't have a ferry. He said go over it. He already had the plan. He already knew how they were going to get over it, but God wants you to have the faith to show up. Throw your hands up and say, "God, I'm showing up this year." Say, "That's why I'm going to get some power. I'm crossing over this. Whatever's in my way, I'm crossing over it."

"...*Thou and all this people.*" (verse 2) Everybody's going. God wants to bless you. Come on. God doesn't only want the pastor to cross over. You're crossing over. You're going to be in that place where everything God said is going to manifest.

"...*Unto the land which I do give to them, even to the children of Israel.*" (verse 2) Look out. Now look at God prophesying on your foot. A pastor woke me up and said, "Come on, Prophet. I want you to go somewhere." He didn't even tell me where I was going. I thought I was going to eat because he used to love that place where we would get fish and grits and eggs. But anyway, he said, "Come on, Prophet."

We drove past the restaurant so, I said well I guess he's going to a new one today. But you see, I'm going to tell the truth. The pastor was spiritual that morning—I wasn't. I was thinking' about my belly. He was talking and I was trying to keep up with him. So, we parked in front of a theater and I saw that the place was full of people. I said, oh my God, we're going to backslide today. I said, "I love him.

We'll just get reclaimed I guess." And he said, "Come on Prophet," because he saw I couldn't figure out what was going on. I knew we were going to pay outside, but he walked right past the ticket taker. I said, "Now we're going to jail." You know, you have to watch the devil. He'll have you operating totally in the flesh. I was totally in the flesh. Now, he didn't tell me he was coming to claim the building. So, I said, "Oh God, we're going to jail."

So, then he walked right down the side of the building. People were looking at us like we were crazy. He was speaking in tongues. I wasn't speaking in tongues. Then he said, "Come on Prophet. Lay hands on this building." Man, I laid hands on the building. It took me about three minutes for that Holy Ghost to hit, because he's praying and I'm mumbling something, but I'm trying to figure out what's going to happen next. But after a while, the Holy Ghost hit me and I said, "Pastor, this is our/your building." He said, "Mine." We were in there hollering, "It's mine. It's mine." Glory to God. And we walked out, and we said, "It's ours."

I learned that day what God meant when He prophesied on your foot. He said every place that your foot shall tread, you can have it, if you believe it. I dare you to stomp your foot and say, "Foot, everywhere you go I will have what God says I'm going to have." Somebody needs to go look at that house tomorrow. Somebody needs to go today and put your foot on that lawn. Use your foot to seal that miracle. Go get it. It's already set up, but you have to have the faith to show up.

The pastor did not have a check book with him. He didn't go see the real estate agent. He came and put his foot on that building. And 30 days later, he said, "Wake up Prophet. Wake up." I said, "What's the matter?" I was sleeping, and he said, "We've got the building." God's ready to manifest it. He's waiting for you to get there.

This is the year that He's going to manifest what the devil thought wasn't going to ever happen. He's going to manifest what people said wasn't going to ever happen. Go get it!

God's got a plan beyond what we can even imagine. It's already set up. And God's getting ready to manifest everything that He ever said. Everything that He ever prophesied. Everything that the devil thought wasn't coming to pass. Every promise. Every prophetic word. It shall come to pass.

And now you must realize you are crossing over and you're going to have what God said because it's getting ready to manifest. In fact, it's already manifested. You've just got to get to the place. It's already released. It's already yours. You have to make up your mind that you're not going to let anybody stop you from crossing over. You're not going to let your flesh stop you. You're not going to let your haters stop you. You're not going to let an attitude stop you. You can have what God said you're going to have. Rise up.

Satan knew if you made it over into 2016, that's this is the year of manifestation. So, he said, "I'm going to wear them out." Have you gone through that wearing out period? Then he said, "I'm going to confuse them. I'm going to make them start wondering why God hasn't done it." Then he said, "I'm going to make them feel like they are by themselves." But all that was a lie. It's your season.

You know, one thing about the devil is if there ever was a fool who didn't know he was a fool, it's the devil. Every time he messes with you God turns around and gives you another miracle. Every time he tries to stop you, God gives you a double miracle. You have to realize something, these people had been in that wilderness for 40 years with promises, with prophesies. But I want you to get that word. It says, "Now." You've been shifted into the now season. You're out of the hope season; you're in the season in which "now" means it's going to come to pass now!

Everything that's been held up is being released. Every door that's been closed is going to open. Every mountain that's been blocking you is going to open. Every situation that's been making you depressed is over. The old people used to sing a song, *'I'm so glad trouble don't last always. I've got a God; I've got a God on my side.'* I don't care what it looks like; you're in 2016, and you're going to have what God said you're going to have. Connect your faith for the season that you're in. God's going to take care of everything. Everything!

Now, here they are, and He said, *"Cross over Jordan."* You have to cross over some stuff. Sometimes you have to step over some people. Whatever you have to step over, step over it so you can get to the place of manifestation.

Joshua told the people, before we go any further, you have to sanctify yourselves. Sanctification means you have to clean up. Sometimes we want the blessings, but we don't want to clean up. Sometimes you have to empty out stuff. Empty out hurt. Empty out failure. Empty out mistakes. And once they did that, they went over on dry ground. The wall of Jericho fell down. (Joshua 6:20) They didn't need a bulldozer or dynamite! They just marched. I dare you to keep marching and watch the walls in your life fall.

You are in a season of manifestation. Before you get to that promised land, you're going to have to deal with a Jordan. You're going to have to deal with a wall of Jericho, but it doesn't matter. The same God who let you survive the wilderness will let you survive whatever the devil has set up. I serve notice on every devil from here to hell that he will not stop the people of God! God is empowering them with faith. He is empowering them with an anointing. They will not be stopped!

Everything that God has for you is in the process of manifestation. It's going to happen. It does not mean that there aren't going to be any more challenges. There will be, but that doesn't even matter. You've been shifted into a place of victory and manifestation. So, whatever the devil got set up, it doesn't even matter, because God's going to give you power.

When God speaks a word, people hear it, but sometimes they don't allow their faith to connect to it. You have to realize that God said this is a season of manifestation. That means that God is going to manifest everything, but you have to believe.

Now, one thing Satan does is come to bluff you and say, "Aww, they said that last year." You notice, he loves to tell us what God said and then try to make us believe it's not going to happen. God said the season is already here. He didn't say it was coming! Joshua said, "*Now!*" And God is telling many of you, "Now!" Now is your time. Now is your season. Now is your hour. Now is your year.

Wherever there is faith, there's got to be some action. Joshua said, "We're not going to have another meeting. We're not going to talk about how we're going to get over." He said, "Now." He told the elders to tell the people to get ready. Are you ready to cross over? Are you ready to have what God says? Or do you have to have another meeting?

Have you ever heard people say, "Well, what's wrong with me? You know what's wrong with you. You know what's wrong and you know what pleases God. Some people treat God like most of us do the gas station. You know, I have a friend and she was one of the drivers in the ministry — a sweet child and full of the Holy Ghost but she didn't have enough to keep her tank full. She always drove on a quarter of a tank or less. You don't know when you're going to run out, and what if there's a traffic jam? Sometimes the red light would be beeping and I'd say, "Daughter, you got... and she would respond, "Oh, I know my car."

How many people are like that? You come to church, the altar's there, the preacher makes the altar call, but you never go. You know that you are on less than a quarter tank. The red light is beeping. But you drive on. Don't start the year like that. You have to get power. Make up your mind that you're not going to let anything stop you from crossing over to your place of manifestation.

God is getting ready to manifest every word that has been spoken over your life. I don't care if it was 10 years ago, 15 years ago, 20 years ago, or yesterday; God said I'm going to manifest every word that's been spoken over your life and it's coming to pass. It's getting ready to happen. It's already in progress, and no devil can stop it. And you know the good thing about it is that when God speaks a word over your life, that word can be tested. That word can go through some fire. That word can go through some dark times. That word is able to stand harassment from the devil. That word might be tested in some turbulent times, but it's still going to happen. You cannot give up. You have to get your faith up. I don't care what you've been through. I don't care what the devil said or what he's done, it's going to happen.

Everything that God said about me is already happening. I've been through the storm, but it's already happening. I might have been knocked out, but I'm up. You haven't seen anything yet! It's happening right now. Manifestation! Stuff that I forgot about. Stuff that my haters thought wasn't going to ever happen. They'd better look again, because God is doing a new thing. I see my miracle. Why don't you open your eyes and see what the

Lord is doing for you? Stop worrying about what folks are saying.

Wake your faith up and open your eyes to see what the Lord is doing. See what He's doing for your son. See what He's doing for your children. See what He's doing in your body. See what He's doing in your finances. See what He's doing with your life. The devil thought you would have been finished by now. The devil thought you would've given up by now. The devil thought you'd have been dead by now but open your eyes and see what God is doing.

See some stuff that the doctor doesn't think is going to happen. See yourself healed and start speaking the word. Say, "I'm healed in the name of Jesus. I am free from that disease and from medicine." When you start seeing it, it starts manifesting.

If you're not saved, if you're a backslider, tell the devil, "You've held me back long enough. You held me down." There comes a time in all of our lives that we've got to make a decision. Lift your hands and close your eyes and say, "Lord Jesus, here I am. Save me today. Deliver me. I accept you now as my Lord, my Savior, my deliverer, and my keeper. I surrender my life to You. God, I thank You for saving me. God, I thank You for delivering me and setting me free."

# Chapter 14
# The Release Is On

No matter what it looks like, my faith is working in every area of my life. And where there is faith, there will always be a challenge, a threat, some form of test, or some situation for which you will have to believe God. God never asked you to help Him. He only asks you to believe in Him and trust in Him. You have to get your faith to that level where you know He's going to do it. You don't know how, but you know that He's going to do it. In spite of what you're already dealing with, a miracle is already released. You have to realize that God already has it worked out, but He just wants you to get there. We talk about it, but we never connect to it. We talk about it, but we never take any action.

Blind Bartimaeus would have still been blind and still been a beggar had he not gotten up and taken action. He got up and began to cry out, *'Jesus, thou Son of David, have mercy on me'* (Mark 10:46—52) When he started crying out, there was opposition. The opposition doesn't matter. We're in a season in which our faith is working—not just talking but working.

In Mark 9:23, God gives us a great formula for a miracle. And 40 years ago, when I was a young preacher, people were afraid to preach about faith because they were trying to tie it in and say that it was nothing but positive thinking. But God opened our eyes to see that faith was His Word. And if you believe His Word, you will see that nothing is impossible. But then you must get it in your spirit that your faith is working. You must get it in your spirit that God has given every man and woman a measure of faith. You have enough faith to get a miracle. The Bible says in Romans 12:3 that God has given every man a measure of faith. The measure of faith is enough faith to get you a miracle wherever you are. Whatever you're going through, you have to begin to program yourself, and begin to tell yourself, "I have enough faith to get a miracle right here."

The Hebrew boys thrown in the fiery furnace testified before they went in. What have you been saying about what God can do? They said, *"We want you to know that our God is able. And if He doesn't do it, we want you to know that He's able."* (Daniel 3:17) He can turn fire into an air conditioner. God can bring about a revolutionary change just like that! This is the season of miracles!

Mark 9:23 says, *"Jesus said, if thou canst believe."* Here it is; this is the formula. Now, when I was in school, the word, "if" was a preposition. "If" means that you might do it or you might not. One of the number one enemies is the word, "if." Some people say, "I would give if I had..." or "I would be healed if I..." We need to get "if" out of the way! One word can cause a miracle to happen if you believe it. We hear faith. We hear the prophetic. We hear the Word that God gives—the corporate Word to the churches. But everybody doesn't receive.

A pastor who died about a week ago came to my church some years ago and said, "Everybody who gives, God is going to give them a special miracle." Everybody loved that part, but he didn't tell us what he wanted us to give at first. He told us what God was going to do, but when he said that God wanted twenty people to give $1,000.00 by Friday, you could hear a pin drop. One girl stood up and came down to get an envelope. I said to myself, "Where is she going to get a thousand dollars from?" He said to her, "I know you don't have it, but your faith has it and you're going to have it." Your faith's not broke, but you need to connect to your faith. Twenty people finally got in the line. I said to him on the way home, "Don't count on that one, Prophet." He said, "DeCuir, she's going to have it!" He was there from Sunday through Friday and every night he told her that she was going to have it, and I said, "Lord, I don't know where she's going to get it from." Take the limit off of your faith and you can have what God says you can have. She was on welfare and we knew the check time had passed. She didn't have a husband, boyfriend, or rich sugar daddy. That Friday she went to the mailbox and you won't believe this. Discover Card sent her a credit card with a limit of $10,000.00. She hadn't applied for it, but God. Out of her faith came a Discover Card! The first thing she did was call them and say, "Can I get a thousand dollars?' They told her that she could get $10,000.00 if she wanted. Let me tell you, she tore that place up! She said, "I didn't have it, but the man of God told me that I was going to have it." God will create a miracle because of your faith. Faith is the substance of things hoped for, the evidence of things not seen. Faith is the evidence that it's going to happen. You don't see it, but it's going to happen. Out of your faith is coming the miracle that you need. It's already set up.

Jesus said, *"If thou canst believe, all things are possible to him that believeth."* If you can have faith! I believe God. I don't care what's in my pocketbook. My faith is not limited to what's in my pocketbook; my God is working a special miracle NOW. The scripture says, *"Now faith is."* (Heb. 11:22) Because of my faith, a miracle is happening NOW. My body is being healed NOW. My financial increase is going on NOW. My family members are being touched NOW. God is turning some things around NOW.

We've got to get our faith to the now level. We've got to connect it to this word, "all." All things are possible; all you need to do is have faith in God and speak in your spirit that it's happening now. "Now" faith is action faith. You have to realize that if you believe God.

The Lord told me to shake the hand of a man who came to my church and to give him $500.00. To tell the truth, I didn't want to give it to him. I gave him the $500.00 and somebody asked me, "Why did you give him $500.00 and you don't even know him, Pastor?" We have to learn to sow when God tells us to sow. The Lord told me that He was going to bless me in 24 hours. I wasn't in revival, but God.

I had a funeral the next day. Have you ever heard of anybody getting blessed at a funeral? I went to the funeral and preached. I committed the body, and at the graveyard, a man was there who was one of the biggest drug dealers in America at the time, but his sister belonged to my church. So, here he comes, and he says, "Hey Reverend. How are you doing?" I said, "Fine." He said, "My sister told me to come and bless you." I said, "Thank you for the blessing." He shook my hand and gave me a paper bag. I put it in my pocket and didn't think anything of it. Then I said, "Oh my

God! That was a drug dealer. Oh my God! The FBI is watching me." I was scared to death. I put my robe on. I was watching everybody. I said, "Lord, I'm not a drug dealer." Mother Holloway was with me and I said, "Mother, put this bag in your purse." I told her what had happened, and we were going down the expressway and Mother was singing and praying and speaking in tongues. I wasn't praying. I was scared to death. But Mother was praying and pleading the blood. I didn't know if the boy had $5.00 or $10.00 or what, but he said that his sister told him to come and bless me. God had said that He was going to bless me in 24 hours. God's got a way. We ran up the stairs of the church and locked the doors. Mother was praying and she said, "The wealth of the wicked is laid up for the just." (Proverbs 13:22) I hadn't thought about that scripture, but after she said it, I was alright. We counted it and it was $5,000.00 I had to obey God when He said to give it. He already had something set up.

I was prompted to give an $80.00 offering, and I said thank You Lord. There was a woman from Jamaica, who said that she went to sleep, and God told her to find the prophet. She was in California and she said she was going to go and give it to my daughter, but the Lord said, "Go and give this to the prophet." I hadn't seen her in two years. She called my office and spoke to the people who take messages. They called me and told me her name. I said, "I don't know who she is. I'll call her when I get back." When I talked to her on the phone, she spoke in tongues for about eight minutes, but after a while she said that God told her to bless me that day. Remember, I only gave $80.00, but she said, "I'm putting $500.00 in your bank account." What if I hadn't obeyed God? If you sow it, God will grow it. Every seed you sow, God releases another harvest. We preach a lot about faith, but we don't preach enough about faithfulness. Remember this: God is faithful, and when you are faithful you always get double honor. Be faithful with your tithing and faithful with your church attendance. Lock your faith into that one word, "all."

The Release Is On

# Chapter 15

# Deeper Insight into Making Your Mouth Agree with Your Faith Even More

The Bible says we walk by faith and not by sight. (2 Cor. 5:7) Now that is quite a challenge because the enemy uses us to cause us to focus on something negative and we retreat from our position of faith. Once you make a stand, you have to stand right there, and every time you open your mouth SAY, it is going to happen.

Faith works. Faith is a common denominator. Everybody has faith...everybody. My grandson played many tricks on me when he was coming up. He stayed with me from the time he was about three years old until he was grown. He would say what he heard me say at church and whenever he really wanted something he would say, "I believe God." I said, "What do you want now?" Because I learned the little game. He would say, "Pawpaw. I believe God." He played this game on me from the time he was about five years of age. Whenever he wanted me to go to McDonald's he would sing two songs, *I believe God, I believe God, I believe God.*' He'd sing it about two blocks, then he'd sing, '*Old MacDonald, Old MacDonald, Old MacDonald.*' He would not ask me, but he programmed me and finally when I got to McDonald's I would inadvertently automatically turn into McDonald's. You know what he would say once he got his sandwich? "Pawpaw, I was praying that you would turn into McDonald's." He was so into faith, he believed it. You've got to get right there... right there where you believe what you say. If we can get there, we're going to have what God said.

I could tell you experiences that I've had. A pastor brought me to a building before the congregation obtained it. He said, "DeCuir, this is Bethel." I said, "Okay." He saw what I didn't see. He told me how many people were going to be in there and all I saw was what I was looking at. I did not see the people, but he did. I didn't see the pulpit. He was telling me about a school and where he was going to put it. Later, everything he stated with his mouth, I saw with my eyes. You have got to realize that God honors the words that come out of your mouth.

I don't care what you say, we put more on the devil than we need to. It's not the devil; it's our mouths. Start saying what God says, what the Word says. Stop saying, "Well, I don't think I'm going to make it. Well, I'm getting old." My mama told me some years ago that nothing gets old but clothes, and she said if you live long enough, they get young again; they come back around. So, start saying what it is, what God says it is. Your mouth... our mouths... are our problem. If we ever line that mouth up, we're going to see miracles.

You have to have discipline. You have to learn. That's why you need the Holy Ghost. The Holy Ghost will tell you to hush. Has the Holy Spirit ever told you to hush now, you talk too much? You know, one day I heard my grandson say something profound—and I can tell you a thousand stories about my grandson. One of the members disturbed me. Sometimes the Israelites get out of hand. And so, I was just going up one side of this member and down the other, and my grandson was standing there looking. So, when he got home, he said, "Pawpaw, you needed to hush today." I said, "What did you say? You don't tell old people they need to hush." I said, "What do you mean?" He said, "Pawpaw, that lady upset you and you were just... you should have hushed." I said, Lord he is telling the truth. I said, "Go on in there and watch TV, boy." What I'm saying is sometime your mouth can hold up and mess up your miracle.

Mark 11 says, *"For verily I say unto you that whosoever shall say ..."*—in other words speak it. After you get through praying, you have to say something. *"Whosoever shall say to this mountain be thou removed and be cast into the sea and shall not doubt in his heart but shall believe that those things which he said shall come to pass, he shall have whatsoever he sayeth.*" If I can say it, I can have it. You have to believe what you say.

Jesus said, "*Whosoever shall say ....*" The mountain, of course, is a symbol of situations. Now, if you don't let your words come in agreement with your faith then you'll be defeated on every purpose. I've learned some things about faith.

God is such a wonderful God that all you have to do is get at the right place and the miracle is waiting on you. All you have to do is get there. I have seen God work little miracles with money. So, I needed $3,000.00 and I tried to raise it with those Israelites and they weren't giving it. I said, "Lord, I need $3,000.00" And the Lord said, "Go to the restaurant." Well where am I going to find $3,000.00 at the restaurant? I only had $5.00 and that couldn't buy a steak. I had to buy some ice cream and soup or salad or something. So, I go in there, sit down to eat, and said, "Lord, really... what am I here for?" All you have to do is be at the right place at the right time. A man came over to me and he said, "Preacher, don't I know you?" I said, "Well..." I couldn't say. He said, "You look like George Jefferson." And I'm like, "God you told me to come here and this man comes with this foolishness." He said, "Well George how's your day?" He's irritating me now, but you have to learn to deal with irritation, because sometimes in that irritation is your miracle. He said, "George, I know you are Pastor DeCuir, but my wife and I watch you." I was on television then every Sunday afternoon. He said, "We watch you every Sunday afternoon and my wife gets really excited when you go to shouting." And he said, "Oh man, she would give you the world if she could when you shout." I wanted to ask where she was so I could give her a shout right now. He said, "And we were just sitting there talking about you. We have been watching you. We are from Germany and have never been to a black church." I said, "Well, you're welcome to come to mine. Mine is all black." I told him like it was. He said, "Well, my wife is fearful because your church is kind of on the borderline." I said, "My church is only four blocks from the Rose Bowl." He said, "Yeah, but on the other side of the Rose Bowl." I said, "Well Sir, you're welcome." And he went on and I'm sitting there like ...God sent me here for a miracle and he didn't have me come here for me to be harassed by this man.

Before I'd known anything, the man came back and picked up my check. When he picked it up, I said, "It's only $4.00 and some cents." He said, "I'm going to take care of your check." I said, "Fine." He said, "I went out to the car to call my wife." When he said wife, I knew the miracle was coming. He said, "My wife told me we must make a donation to you today." I heard him the first time, but I said "When?" because I needed $3,000.00. He said, "My wife said do it today, to bless you today." And I was just sitting there like I wasn't watching but he was writing. Glory to God! I started thanking God when I saw him write that three, hallelujah! I knew it was going to be $3,000.00. That man wrote a check for $3,900.00. See, you have to believe and do what God says. Learn to do it. Just do what He says.

# Chapter 16

# My Faith Is Working Now

Whenever I speak at the School of Faith, something happens to my faith, and I leave like a spiritual Superman, knowing that God can do anything. God can do anything that you have the faith to believe that He can do. The Bible declares that without faith, it is impossible to please God. In this faith situation, the Bible declares that faith is a common denominator among all. So, you have it whether you use it or not. Most of us have faith that we don't do anything with. Where there's faith, there's got to be some action. If there is no action, there will be no miracle.

It takes faith. We have to break the barrier of everybody else doing well, except us. If some can raise $100,000.00 on a Sunday morning, why can't other people? You have to learn to name your seed. We talk a lot about faith, but we don't talk about faithfulness. God is going to celebrate you because you have been faithful. You are faithful with your tithe. Faithful with your giving. Faithful with your holy living. Faithful with your commitment. Faithful to your leader. God keeps records of your faithfulness and He doesn't overlook them. God says He will honor your faithfulness.

When you take action, God takes action. When you move, God moves. Faith is knowing that God is going to do it. We need to learn that God honors faithfulness... I believe God.

I've got a son named Jon Jon. Ever since he was a kid, he loved to go to the radio station. I did a broadcast in Los Angeles for 15 years every night from 12 midnight 'til 2:00 am in the morning, and here is Jon as a little boy about 2 years old saying, "I want to go with Daddy." I would say, "Bring him on." And he would go to the station. He could say, 'I believe God' before he could say, 'Daddy.' I would be doing the broadcast and he would be saying, "I want to talk. I want to talk." I'd say, "Well, Jon Jon wants to talk." And Jon would say, "I believe God." I would try to take the mic and he would say, "No." His mother would have to take him because he was going to cut up if he couldn't keep the mic. As Jon grew up, I watched God work miracles for him. He's smart, just like his father.

I'm a faith preacher and I live by faith. So, when it came time for Jon to graduate, he wanted to go to one of the big universities. I had a brother-in-law at that time who owned a mortuary in New Orleans; one of the biggest black owned mortuaries there. They were millionaires. They used to come out to visit us when Jon was about 10 years old, and my brother-in-law would say, "Prophet, are you saving any money for Jon to go to school?" I'd say, "Well, I'm working on it." Finally, he came one year, and I went to the bank and put $25.00 in a savings account for Jon to go to school. He asked, "Prophet, do you have a bank account yet?" I said, "Oh yeah." He said, "How much do you have?" I said, "Well, I'm not going to tell you how much I've got." He had a daughter for whom he had to pay $90,000.00 for her to go to Grambling University. And Jon's mother said, "Well, we'll just send him to the junior college." I said, "He's going to the university." Jon came in and said, "Dad, I know you live by faith. I'll just go to the junior college." I said, "Jon, you're going to the university." He looked at me and said, "Daddy?" I used my faith, and I said, "Lord, I know You're going to send my boy to the university."

A pastor came to my church and asked people to give $500.00. In my heart, I said, "Lord, I'm giving this $500.00 for Jon to go to the university." I didn't tell Jon. I didn't tell anybody. I didn't worry about it, and they all thought Jon was going to the junior college. Then the pastor called me and said, "Reverend, I'd like to talk to you." I said to myself, "I know my faith is working." He said, "Reverend, I have five kids that I have to give minority scholarships to—full scholarships. There have to be two

Hispanics and two Blacks. Would you mind if Jon were one of those children? He has the grades. All you'd have to do is buy hamburgers. They will pay for everything." Do you know that my son graduated from Berkeley University and all I had to do was buy hamburgers? God's already got it set up. All he wants you to do is show up with your faith.

When Jon got out of school, he went to work for the city for a while. Then the largest African American church in Pasadena hired Jon to be the Administrator and Associate Pastor. He wanted a Mercedes, but he said he couldn't be paying $500.00 or $600.00 a month. He said, "I'm going to do what my daddy does. I'm going to believe God."

There was a Chinese girl who attended that church. She had asked Jon to come and pray for her father who was dying and going to be with the Lord. She didn't ask Jon to pray that he not die. She wanted him to pray for him before he went to heaven. Jon went over and prayed and everyone there was thankful. The next day, the man went to heaven. Three weeks later, they called Jon over. They were nice to him and they were thanking him. They said, "Jon, Daddy has two cars outside. One is a Lexus and one is a Mercedes. One has 13,000 miles and the other has 20,000 miles. Pick whichever car you want." Paid in full. God's got a miracle set up for you, but you have to show up with your faith. Just use your faith. A miracle is going to happen.

Faith is expecting. When you release your faith, you have to look for it. You have to start saying it. The words of your mouth have to confirm. The words of your mouth can either confirm your faith or destroy your faith. If you believe God for healing, you have to say, "I am healed."

I said to a woman in Las Vegas, "What do you want God to do?" She said, "I want a husband." I said, "Everybody who doesn't have a husband wants one." She said, "Pastor, I've been wanting a husband for five years." She said, "I want a saved man." Get what you want and don't accept anything less than what you want. I told her to go home and start praising God for your husband. I told her to get a pillow with her name on it, and another pillow, and tell that pillow, 'goodnight' every night. She says she did it for three days and she told her friend, "Girl, I told my husband 'goodnight.'" Her friend asked, "What's his name?" She said, "I don't know." She told her friend about how she came to the meeting and the Prophet told her to start telling her husband goodnight. Then one morning she looked over at the pillow and said, "Honey, I will see you when I get home from work." Her sister called her about a month later and asked her, "Are you still talking to the pillow?" She said, "I'm going to talk to him until he comes."

I went back to Vegas and saw her and her sister. Her sister said, "Prophet, you have her talking to a pillow. We think we're going to have to commit her. Since you said her husband was coming, will you please tell her when he's coming?" I said, "Soon." That word came out of my mouth. She was a schoolteacher. At work one day the maintenance man came in to clean up. A little boy had messed up everything with paint and she had to tell him what to do. As he was cleaning up, he asked her, "Do you go to church?" She said, "I'm saved, sanctified, and filled." He said, "Since you're saved and I'm saved, I want you to go to church with me." She said, "I have my own church." He said, "Well, I'll go with you." She told him, "I didn't ask you to go to church." He said, "Aren't you supposed to bring souls to church?" She said, "Sir, you go to your church and I'll go to mine." She said all night long her spirit was troubled, and when she got to school the next morning, she went to him and said, "Sir, please forgive me. You're welcome to come to my church." He said, "Well, I'll come." He went to her church and her sister teased her afterwards. She said, "The prophet said it." She told her sister, "He's a janitor."

Let me tell you something, one night he came to prayer and they were praying. God got a hold of her and told her that he was going to be her husband. She said she got up from prayer and sat down. She said, "This devil is a lie. The janitor isn't my husband." She didn't tell anybody. Her sister called her and said that she was on the prayer line and the Lord said that the janitor was going to be her husband. She said, "Lord, if that's my husband, let him propose to me."

The man called her and invited her to dinner. She asked him where they were going, and he told her that he wanted to take her to the most expensive place that there was. He took her to this nice place and when he took her home, he asked her if he could come in because he wanted to talk to her. She said, in her heart, she could feel it. He said that God told him that she was his wife when they first met. He told her that he was going to marry her. She asked him when, and he told her since they were in Las Vegas, they could do it now. They got married. If God said it, you should believe it. You have to look beyond what you see.

There was a mother who went to my church and ever since I was her pastor, her leg had been hurting. She had knee trouble. One day she fell down at the market and she said, "I'm going to get $20,000.00." They went to court and she was offered $5,000.00. She came back to church and said, "They're going to give me $20,000.00." Mother went back to the court room with her anointing oil and started anointing chairs. She anointed the chair that the judge sat in, the chairs that the district attorney sat in—she was anointing everything. The bailiff asked her, "What are you doing?" She said, "My case is tomorrow and I'm praying." The bailiff looked at her and said, "Poor thing."

Let people say what they want, but you have to use your faith. Let them say that you're crazy. You have to say, "My faith is working." Mother went to court and finally, the judge said, "Gentlemen, what are we going to do?" talking to the district attorney and the public defender. The district attorney said, "Well, we're not going to settle; she will not agree." The judge said, "You all have dragged this out for the last three years. I'm going to settle it for you and her. He hit down the gavel and said, "Case settled for $30,000.00."

God will reverse it right before the enemy's eyes. What the devil thinks is going to happen will not happen because God will reverse it because of your faith. The Bible says in Romans 1:17, "*The just shall live by faith.*" Faith is working, and I've seen God do the miraculous. Take the limits off your faith.

Mark 2:1 says, "*And again he entered into Capernaum after some days.*" God's going to move again. It's your time again. It's your hour again. You can have what God says you can have. The scripture goes on to say through Verse 5, "*...and it was noised that he was in the house. And straightway many were gathered together,* *insomuch that there was no room to receive them, no, not so much as about the door: and he preached the word unto them. And they come unto him, bringing one sick of the palsy, which was borne of four. And when they could not come nigh unto him for the press, they uncovered the roof where he was: and when they had broken it up, they let down the bed wherein the sick of the palsy lay. When Jesus saw their faith, he said unto the sick of the palsy, Son, thy sins be forgiven thee."*

When Jesus saw their faith, a miracle happened. When my faith is working, a miracle happens. My faith is not dead faith. My faith is not asleep. My faith is not dormant. My faith is not down in the valley; my faith is getting ready to move me to the mountaintop. A miracle is going to happen. Don't ever count anyone out that is believing God. People who walk in faith make miracles happen. Faith can work while you sleep. Sometimes, all people need to do is take a nap. Have you ever heard the illustration about the farmer who sowed a seed and went to sleep? Take a nap and let God work a miracle. Stop worrying and take a nap. Stop being depressed and take a nap. Stop being confused because your faith is working.

# Chapter 17

# God Has It All Under Control

God has it all under control. No matter what it looks like, God's got it all under control. I've learned to just read and say what God says. Sometimes, I have a lot that I want to say, but what I want to say doesn't matter. What matters is what God wants you to hear. The Word says in Numbers 23:19 that *"God is not a man, that he should lie; neither the son of man, that he should repent: hath he said, and shall he not do it? or hath he spoken, and shall he not make it good?"*

I want you to keep in mind some things that God has said about you. Can you remember one thing that God said that He was going to do? Do you believe He's going to do it? He said, *"Behold, I have received commandment to bless: and he hath blessed; and I cannot reverse it."* (Numbers 23:20) I want you to think about what that word is saying. You must get it in your mind that God is well aware of where you are. Because of God, you were able to survive what the devil thought you weren't going to survive. You were able to come through what all the demons of hell never dreamed you were going to come through. God has it all under control.

The scripture says that God is not a man. You know man will put you up today and take you out tomorrow. Whenever you start believing God, and whenever God has spoken a word over your life, that word will be challenged by the devil, but it doesn't even matter. Because of Him and because of His word, you survived everything that you went through. Think back seven years. Has the devil ever tried to take everything including your joy, including your anointing? Has he tried to break up your relationship with God or tried to make you lose confidence in what God said? But you can say that you survived it and you still have a praise.

I still have a praise. I still have relationship. I still have fellowship. I'm still walking in righteousness. I still have a praise.

Everything that God said and everything that God prophesied over your life it's still going to happen. It's already in operation and there is not a demon from here to hell that can stop what God is doing. Nobody. Your haters can't stop what God is doing. Witchcraft can't stop it. Nothing can stop it because it's your season and it's your time. We spend half of our life dealing with what people say, but you have to keep your mind on what God says.

I wonder if you can think of something that God said that He's going to do and you're not backing up on it? I love that verse, which says, *"Behold, I have received commandment to bless: and they are blessed, and I cannot reverse it."* The man thought that if he went to the prophet, the prophet could reverse it. But what God has for me cannot be reversed. I don't care who doesn't want it to happen; it's already set up. It's going to happen. It's already in progress. It's already been released. The prophet said, "I know you want me to curse them." That other fella wanted the prophet to curse them, but I'm trying to get it in your spirit that it doesn't matter what people want. All that matters now is that you know what God said and you stand on that. God said it and I believe it and it's happening right now—everything that your enemies and the devil thought was dead; things that they thought were over. They haven't seen anything yet. You've just entered a season of manifestation, and everything that the devil thought was canceled is getting ready to happen. All will be restored. Everything the devil thought you lost, God's going to give it back double. All will be restored. Speak that word. Your anointing, your faith, everything. Everything will be restored. Your joy. Your commitment. God is telling you to stop worrying about what you lost. God said all will be restored. God prophesied and said 7 years of restoration. God said it. I believe it. It cannot be reversed.

Isaiah 61:7 tells us what God said He's going to do for you who have been faithful, for you who held on when the devil thought you were going to give up, for you when it looked like you were about to go under. It looked like you were at the end but look at what God said He was going to do. *"God is not a man, that he should lie; neither the son of man, that he should repent: hath he said, and shall he not do it? Or hath he spoken, and shall he not make it good?"*

# Chapter 18
# It's Already Released

You're here by divine appointment. God has a plan. God's got a word of faith, and all things are working in your favor. God said something powerful in Luke 10:19. He said, *"I give you power."* Not just power to shout. It doesn't take power to shout, but it takes power to tell the devil that it is not working; it's canceled. We speak a word of faith. Your mouth can mess up everything. Stop saying what the devil wants you to say and start saying what God wants you to say. We get in trouble because we magnify the words of the enemy. Magnify what God says. God works miracles even while you're sleeping. Sleep well because God is working out some things. My faith is working. No matter what the odds say, I know that I'm in the midst of a miracle.

My wife wanted a car. I took her to the car lot, and I thought she was going to choose the Ford, but she passed the Ford and went over to the Lincoln lot and claimed it. I knew that when she got ahold of faith, God was going to deliver it. We are constantly dealing with what people say that we can't have. We thank God for Experian, Equifax, and TransAmerica, but they don't control what God wants you to have.

In 2006 I was pastoring, and a little Hispanic lady said, "Padre, God's going to bless you." Now, I speak very little Spanish, but she said, "El coche." I said, "Car." She said, "Nuevo." I said, "New." I started recollecting the words and she said, "New. Off floor. Nobody ever rode in it, but you." I said, "Thank You Jesus. She said, "Receive it. Ahora!" That came back to my brain. That meant, 'now.' I was running a revival and she was running around the church telling everybody, "Padre is going to get nuevo coche. Ahora!" She came back and said, "Receive it." I said, "God, I can't afford a brand-new car." All night, I could hear her saying, 'now.' The woman said it, but my faith could not connect to what God said. I heard it! I hear it even now! You can hear a word, but that word has to connect with your faith. I was trying to figure out how I was going to get a brand-new car. You do not have to figure out what God's going to do and how He's going to do it. All God needs is your faith and your praise. You don't know who God's going to use to bless you. It's already released.

I went to a meeting to hear a prophetess, but I wasn't preaching. I just went and I gave $1,000.00. The Lord said to give $1,000.00 and when I got to the prophetess, she was telling people what God was going to do. I was ready to receive this long prophecy, but she said, "Prophet, it's done." I wanted to say, "What is done?" She said it with power, and I could feel the anointing. When I woke up the next morning, the Lord said, "The car is yours." But I was still wondering how.

I went to run a revival at a small Baptist church in Lancaster, CA. All I gave was $1,000.00, but you don't know *WHAT* your offering's going to do. So, I was in the Baptist church preaching, and a man about 30 years old said, "Prophet, the Lord told us to buy you a new car." I didn't get very happy, but I should have because God told me it was already done. It's a wonder that God gave me the miracle because I was wondering where this man was going to get the money to buy me a car.

About three Sundays from then, he showed up at my church and said that he wanted to say something when I was finished ministering and prophesying. He said, "I want to talk to the people about this car." I said, "Brother, you don't know this group." They're what I call '*professional saints.*' The man got up and said, "People, the Lord told me to buy Prophet DeCuir a brand-new car off the floor." The people went to clapping and I was looking out of one eye. He said, "I want everybody to get up and pledge $300.00." I put my head down, I felt sorry for him. I said, "poor man." I saw about 30 people get up. He told me that he was going to call me and meet me at the car lot. I started praising God because I knew it was going to happen. That man called me about three days before there was going to be a celebration for me. I met him at the car lot. He said, "Reverend DeCuir, what do you want?" He said, "This is the Lincoln lot here. That is the Jaguar lot over there. That is the Cadillac lot over there." I felt like a little boy. I said, "I want that brand-new Lincoln over there off the floor." I want you to know that I drove away with a brand-new Lincoln, off the floor. For two and a half years, that Baptist church leased the car. I didn't make a payment. I didn't pay for an oil change. I could even go to the dealer and make them wash it. Take the limit off your faith. If God said it, then it's going to happen.

In Mark 5 we read about a woman who was counted out. Death was going to be the ultimate for her, but something happened. Her faith came alive. Wherever there is faith, there will be a challenge. Whenever there is faith, there will be a threat by the devil to make you retreat. Whenever there is faith, the devil will always come with something or somebody to make you lose your position. Once you say that God's going to do it, keep on saying it. You have to say it until you know it. Mark 5:25 says, "*A certain woman ...*" It didn't call her name but it said, a certain woman. Where there is faith, there is power. Where there is faith, there will be no fear. The number one enemy of faith is not the devil. The number one enemy of faith is fear.

Peter did something that no one else had done. He said, *"Lord, if this is you, bid me to come."* Jesus only spoke one word, "Come." (Matthew 14:28-29, 31) Those other disciples stood there looking at Peter. You know what they were saying? "He's going to sink after a while." "Poor Peter. He probably can't swim." But Peter stepped out on a word, "Come." There is power in the word of God. Peter started walking down the road of faith. Peter got distracted. The devil will create a distraction. The same water was there, but Peter looked around and saw the waves rolling and the wind blowing. He started focusing on what he saw, and not on what he heard. Peter started sinking and the people started saying that he was sinking. You see, people love to magnify your failures. Jesus told Peter to take His hand. There was no boat to get Peter, but when the disciples looked again, Peter was walking on the water with Jesus. You're not going under because your faith is working. Your miracle is coming.

It's Already Released

# Chapter 19

# Have Faith

God's schedule is not your schedule. You will always have a choice to do it your way, but that's how we get into trouble; we have a choice. You will find out that God is not Burger King. You can't have it your way. Your way may be the easiest way, but it doesn't mean that it's God's way. One of my friends said that every door is not a God door. That was deep to me. Sometimes you want to do it your way, but it might not be God's way.

God knows the tests that you will encounter, and the one way that you will be ready for the test is that your faith will have to be at a certain level. People don't realize that sometimes we're not ready for the challenge. This is why we have to constantly build our faith. You have to be able to say, "My faith is working."

We read the Bible and we hear preachers preach, but do we really let the Bible become a part of our lives and work in our lives? The Bible says in Romans 1:17, "*As it is written, the just shall live by faith.*" One of the interpretations says that the just shall walk by faith. When it says that the just shall live by faith, it literally means that for God's people, things turn around because of their faith. Where there is faith, there will be miracles and victories that the devil doesn't think is going to happen. When you look back on your life and your faith was at the right level, there were miracles that God did that were not supposed to happen. You read about people in the Bible like the woman with the issue of blood, but what about your faith? Is your faith working? Can you name examples in your life in which you can say surely, I know my faith will work? You have to be able to say, "I know it works." I read about Paul. I read about Peter, but I know that mine is working. Many times, we forget that the same God who did it before will do it again. God's going to do it. It's already in progress.

Faith is a common denominator among all men. Everybody's got faith. Sometimes we spend half of our lives as believers, using someone else's faith, and never using our own. Wouldn't the world be better if we had enough faith, not only for ourselves, but to help somebody else? We are so used to having faith for ourselves, but nobody else. We have self-faith. Faith is like giving. When you give it, you receive it. Also, when you put faith to work, you get a blessing.

I have a friend who is a Methodist preacher. We went to school together, and he loves this faith thing. He said, "DeCuir, I could just hear you preach faith for days."

So, I went over there. They had about 200 members. I said, "If you put your faith to work, you will have 2,000 members." I said, "God's going to take this church from 200 to 2,000 IF you put your faith to work." Guess what? They're on their way. They have 1,500, and all they did was start inviting people to church. They have about three services going on now on a Sunday morning. Their pastor is a very intellectual man, but he didn't do it. He says they put their faith to work and started inviting people, and people started inviting people. If Donald Trump can round up thousands of people to follow him through social media, what could believers do if we would put social media to work with our faith? He took advantage of the techniques of social media and now look where he is.

You don't have faith just to say that you have faith. You have faith for God to work miracles and for God to do something in your life and for others. Some people have a credit card with a limit of $50,000.00, but they never use it. I have a friend with $250,000.00 worth of credit in his wallet, but he won't even use it to buy a hamburger. He refuses to use the credit cards. He'd rather live at a level of lack than to use that credit card. He'll let you buy dinner or fill his car up with gas. That's the way some people are about faith. Use your faith.

Matthew 17:20 says, *"And Jesus said unto them, Because of your unbelief: for verily I say unto you, If ye have faith as a grain of mustard seed, ye shall say unto this mountain, Remove hence to yonder place; and it shall remove; and nothing shall be impossible unto you."* Faith as small as the size of a mustard seed will give the devil fits. It will give him a nervous breakdown and mess up his plan. We don't realize that faith is one of the weapons that God gave us. God has given every man a measure of faith. A measure is just enough to get you the miracle that you need. We don't realize that we have it. We hear testimonies of others, but we have to realize that we have it. We hear testimonies from others that should encourage us, but we'll say things like, "God doesn't bless me. God doesn't ever give me a financial miracle." This is because we don't bring our faith to that level.

A woman heard me preach about using your faith. She lived in the borderline hood. There were about five Sundays when I preached on nothing but faith. I said, "Everybody who wants a miracle, come to the five services." Everybody was coming. People who weren't saved were coming and they got saved. And here comes this woman. I told her, "I want you to claim a house this morning." She had no credit. She didn't have bad credit; she had no credit. She had God and she had faith. I said, "I want you to give

God the biggest bill that you have." She had a 20-dollar bill, a 50-dollar bill, a 100-dollar bill, and a 10-dollar bill. So, she tried to play God and she dropped the 50-dollar bill in. I said, "Is that the biggest one?" She said, "No, Prophet." I said, "God said give the biggest one." She went back and brought the 100-dollar bill. Now, I have a deacon who is very humorous, and as she was standing there, he said, "What you want?" She said, "I want my $50.00 back." He said, "Don't you hear Pastor preaching about faith?" They were carrying on kind of jokingly and I said, "Hey, you are interrupting me." She said, "Pastor, I'm sorry." The deacon said, "Well, if God doesn't bless you, I'm going to double it." She said, "Alright, I know where you live." I told her to go that afternoon and claim her house. She said, "Whoo-hoo, I know where it is." And she started shouting and the deacon started laughing. She told him, "Laugh all you want, I'm going to have that house." So, that lady went to this house up on a hill with her sister, and she said that she was going to shout on the front lawn. Her sister said, "Girl, you're going to go to jail." This was the kind of neighborhood where you didn't do something like that. She went out and started praising God, and a couple of people were looking at her, and she said, "It's mine." She came back and testified about the house and the address, and the deacon said, "Ummph. Ummph. Ummph!" He was trying to say that there was no way she was getting that house. She said, she didn't care what anybody said. She didn't know how much the house cost.

When your faith is working, the cost doesn't matter. I was still preaching, and I told them that sometimes you have to go back and confirm what your faith has already said was yours. I told them that the next day was Monday and to go back to confirm and say that it was theirs. She went back to the same house and when she was there, the young lady who owned the house was there. The young lady looked at her and listened to her real good, and while she was talking, a young man showed up. They were husband and wife and were planning a divorce. God knows how to bring a miracle for you out of a bad situation. She started praying for them.

One of them wanted to sell the house and one of them wanted to keep it. The young lady said, "I'm tired of this house being empty. We've got to do something. You know what I'm going to do?" The young man said, "What are you going to do? I'm part of this house, too." The young lady reached in her pocket and gave her the key and told her to take the keys and move into the house until they got their business straight, and all she needed to do was pay the water bill. God will create an unusual miracle for you. She came back to the church and said, "These are the keys that you thought I wasn't going to get." She looked at the deacon and said, "See Deacon, my faith is working." She moved into the house with her children. For a year and a half, we had all of the church functions and dinners at her house because it was that kind of house. She had the furniture, refrigerator, beds, and all of the TVs that were already there and all she had to pay was the water bill. Time went by. She kept the place spotless. The couple would stop by from time to time and she would witness to them. She said, "Well Lord, it's been good, but I guess I've got to give it up." Don't release what God gave you.

The young man and young lady came to the house and said that they wanted to talk to her. They said, "You prayed for us and we're no longer getting a divorce. We went to church and got saved." They were both lawyers. They told her that they had to do something with the house, but they figured out a way that she could have the house. She had disqualified herself because she said she couldn't get a loan, but when God set it up, He set up everything.

The young lady said, "My brother is the vice president of Family Savings Bank and I've already talked to him. We're going to give you $25,000.00 for the down payment." They gave her $25,000.00 and she went down to Family Savings Bank of Los Angeles which is now United Bank, and the banker asked her, "Have you ever been a receptionist?" She said, "No." He said, "We need a receptionist. Would you take the job?" She said, "Yes Sir." In one day, she got a house, a job, $25,000.00, and guess what? She's now married to the vice president of the bank. God can do the miraculous in one day.

Whenever I do meetings in Los Angeles, she comes, and when she gives an offering, she says, "One day." She went from the ghetto to the palace and all she did was sow.

# Chapter 20

# My Faith Is Working

In order for faith to work, you have to say, "Yes, Lord." You can't be running from stuff. God has not given you the spirit of fear. You have faith to go through everything. The devil is a fool and he's the only fool that doesn't know that he's a fool. Every time he messes with us, The Lord already knows what the devil's going to do. God already has a prearranged miracle, and all you have to say is, "I believe God." It isn't my business how, but I know that God's going to fix it.

A little baby can't talk. He can't tell his mama that he wants milk. He can't tell his mama to change his diaper, but you know what he can do? He can say, "Aaah.... aaah." And if she doesn't move in a hurry, he can say, "Aaah. Aaah. Aaah!" And the moment she comes to pick him up and give him that bottle, he says, "Mmm." When you need God, just give Him a praise. Whenever you need God, do like the baby and yell out, Hallelujah!

There are so many areas of faith, and so many don't realize that faith and praise are connected. After you release your faith, all you have to do is praise. I dare you to praise Him.

God has designated places for us. God told Elijah that He had a miracle already set up. He said, *"I want you to go down to the brook Cherith, and when you get there, I have commanded the ravens to feed you there."* (1 Kings 17:3-4) Raven is a nice name for what we in the country used to call a buzzard. And a buzzard is nothing but a scavenger who looks out for himself only. But God told Elijah to go down to the brook. Don't go down there looking for Burger King. Don't go down there looking for McDonald's. Don't go down there looking for Bozo's and Popeyes. But I've got an order. I've got a command that I'm getting ready to do. I'm going to command the ravens to feed you there. God is going to command doors to open. He's going to command people to bless you. He's going to command your son or daughter to be loosed. He's going to command promotion on the job. My faith is working.

In Charlotte, North Carolina, I told a girl that God was going to create a miracle for her. She said, "I need one." I said, "Before the month is over, God is going to bless you." She didn't own her grandma's house, but she lived in it. Her grandma had gone to heaven and the rest of the family were fussing.

Then they told her to just stay in the house. One of the brothers came over and told her to take all of the junk that grandma had in the garage and sell it and keep everything. She called her boyfriend and told him what her uncle said. The boyfriend noticed something and said, "Look over at all of those coins. Girl, those coins are worth something. They're antique." She didn't know, but God had planned a miracle. She later testified that she had $89,000.00. God will make a miracle happen. What the devil meant for evil, God will turn it around. Receive it by faith. God's got it all in control.

The Bible says that the just shall live by faith. What that means is that the just people who are walking in expectancy, people who are living by faith are people who know that God is going to fix it. The old folks used to sing a song that says, '*Ain't none of my business how the Lord's gon' fix it. I only know He's gonna fix it.*' Don't worry about it. God's going to fix it. You can put on your shouting shoes. You can put on your praise garments. It's already done in the name of Jesus. Reach up and grab your miracle and receive it.

My grandson, Mister, jumped up and gave an offering when he was about three years old. He heard me talking about giving and he gave around a dollar. He came to me a week later and he wanted some Nike's. I said I wasn't going to buy any expensive shoes. He said, "I want those shoes, Papaw. They cost a lot of money." He said, "Papaw, when you give, God blesses you with what you want, doesn't He?" I said, "Oh yeah." He said, "I know He's going to bless me with those shoes." He put the Word on me. Put the Word with your faith and know that God's going to do it. The Word says that whatsoever things you desire, when you pray, believe that you received them, and you shall have them. (Mark 11:24) Watch God move.

On February 5, 2015 I got up in my church and resigned from my position as pastor. My faith was up, but the moment I resigned, my faith went down. However, God has met every one of my needs. I was used to working with a Sunday morning offering. When that was eliminated, my faith had to go to another level. But do you know that I'm glad because I'm learning about God. God will show you that He is your provider, your sustainer, your way maker. God will show you, and everybody will know that He is on your side. He will show you that He is your God; He will provide. Raise your expectancy level.

In April, after I had resigned, I was sitting in my church. I needed a miracle. The Lord told me to go outside, so I walked outside. I was going back inside and one of my members, one who seems like she never has any money ever, said, "Prophet, can I see you for a minute?" I said,

"Yes." She said, "You're not the pastor anymore, but you're the overseer." I said, "Yes." I wanted to tell her that I would be the bishop or whoever I needed to be. I knew a miracle was coming. She said, "I've been wanting to give you this for two months." She shook my hand and I said, "Thank you, Daughter." The devil said, "It's only $5.00" I went back in and said, "Excuse me; I've got to go to the bathroom." I had to go see what it was. When I went in there, they heard me holler out, "Glory." I went in there and had a praise up in there. That girl shook a thousand dollars in my hand. God will create money miracles. That's why you have to give Him glory. That's why you have to stop worrying. God told us in His Word that He would supply every one of our needs. Look for unexpected miracles from unusual places.

Jeremiah 32:27 says, *"Behold, I am the LORD, the God of all flesh: is there anything too hard for me?"* Get it in your mind that God knows where you are, and He knows what you need. He's already got it set up. God will give you rest from the press. God will give you rest from stress. Stop worrying about it and rest on the Word. The children of Israel took a three-day rest when they were going to cross over. There is nothing too hard for God. Your situation is just right for God to work a miracle. God knows where you are right now. He's already prearranged it. Even when

Moses got to the Red Sea, it was prearranged. God could have opened the sea the night before, but as they were marching, somebody said, "Don't turn around. You will never guess who. It's Pharaoh." Don't panic. You're on the brink of a miracle. They saw the Red Sea and they saw Pharaoh, and they disconnected themselves from the miracle. They began to complain. They forgot all that God had done. But God will show you and the devil that He is God. In the midst of their panic, they received an order from God—stand still. Then He told them to hush. Shut up. Hush. Hush and let God work the miracle. Sometimes we will take a stand on faith, but because of what we see, we will panic and say that God isn't moving, but don't abandon your miracle.

# Chapter 21

# Every Seven Days

I hear the word, *"flush out."* The Lord said that some of the diseased cells that are trying to form in your body are going to flush out. Don't fear anything. You are a child of the King. What the devil meant for evil, God has already turned into a miracle. God said, some things are turning around right now. They're reversing right now. They're being canceled right now. You're being set up. All you have to do is fast—sometimes 7 days, sometimes 14 days, sometimes 20 days, sometimes 40 days. God's got some things that He wants to do for you. He's got us in a process every 7 days. The number 7 is a cycle. Every seven days God is going to do something miraculous. God's going to do something that the devil thought wasn't going to be done. Every 7 days a stronghold is going to move. Every 7 days a door is going to open. Every 7 days it's going to be another season of release.

I want somebody to get that in your spirit. Every 7 days God's going to honor you. Every 7 days God's going to release something. Every 7 days God is going to move something out of your way. I prophesy, by this time next week, you're going to see that God has done another miracle in your life. By this time next week, somebody is going to get a breakthrough. Praise God for your miracle. Whatever is in your way, God's going to move it out of your way. Whatever it is that has been holding you down, nothing will be able to hold you down. Whatever has been blocking you, between now and next week, you're going to see that God has done another miracle in your life.

God, open their eyes that they might see that they're not just going hungry, but you're moving things. You're changing things. You're pulling down strongholds. You're moving the mountains. You're opening up the Red Sea. God, let them step over what the devil thought was holding them up. Give them the strength to rise up and go over their Jordan.

Rise up! You're ready to GO over that Jordan. You're ready to move that mountain. You don't have to climb it. It's going to be moved out of the way. This is the season. Rise up and step over some stuff. There is an anointing that has been released, and it's the anointing that breaks yokes. It is the anointing that moves mountains. It's the anointing that's pulls down strongholds. It's the anointing that gives you power.

We've been in the wilderness experience long enough, but now we're rising up! Come on! Let's rise up!

We have to go get our stuff. We have to go get our heritage. We have to go get our legacy.

I have survived disaster, but I'm now in the midst of victory! I have to make a move now. I have to connect now. I have to let the word come forth in me now.

The Bible says after the death of Moses, the servant of the Lord, the Lord spoke to Joshua, the son of Nun and said, "Arise and go into the land which I promised you." What God was really saying was Moses is dead but my word isn't. My prophecies are not dead. I don't care what you're going through; every word that God has spoken over your life is getting ready to manifest.

I can hear the Lord telling somebody rise up! He said, *"Now therefore arise."* In other words, He said, I know Moses is dead; I know you're grieving. Stop grieving. What's done is already done. Stop worrying about it. The devil's got you wondering about stuff. You know, all the devil can do it's talk about old stuff because he's not a creator. God has a plan that the devil doesn't even know about. God has some miracles that the devil hasn't even known about. God has your record and He sees your faith, and He sees your faithfulness. He sees you pressing. He sees you holding on. You're going to be glad you've held on.

Have you ever noticed that if you live long enough, there are things that happen in our lives that are supposed to make you turn your back on God? Sometimes you get hurt. Maybe you get hurt in your marriage or get hurt in church. Sometimes you get hurt by your children, but God knew it was going to happen.

A lady came to me once who had a son who went to jail. He was a good boy, but they put him in jail for 5 years. When the lady came to me, she said, "I was a good mother." She was saying, I was this and I was that, and I sat there at my desk looking up at the sky. When she got through, I said, "God knew it was going to happen, but God's got a plan." She didn't even know that her son was a member of a gang and the other gang said they were going to kill them all. Her son was on the hit list. God had a plan. God locked him up! God's got a plan and you might not understand it, but the plan is working. The boy was in jail three years. He got saved in the jailhouse. He called his momma and said, "Momma, I'm saved!" He started preaching in the jailhouse. God's got a plan and He's going to do what He's got to do.

The boy came out preaching and she brought him to me. She said, "Pastor told me God allowed it." He said, "God did allow it, because if I would have been out [of jail], I would have been dead."

Now the Word says, "Now *after the death of Moses...*" I used to hear testimonies and some questions would go through my mind. I used to hear preachers say that they met somebody and that somebody gave them a bunch of money, but it had never happened to me.

One day I was going to Fort Lauderdale, Florida. I was with a young man and we were late and I thought I missed my flight. I didn't want to go but the Lord said go. When I got there the attendant said, "You're alright. The flight is an hour late." So, I was on time. The devil thinks you missed it. You haven't missed anything. When I got on the plane, there was a precious Caucasian lady, and this was when they let all the old people go first. She had her walker and it was a long line. I decided that I didn't want to be in the line I was in, so I got right behind her. I didn't know how old she was, and the man said, "You look mighty young to be behind this lady." I told him, "Don't let looks fool you." She was taking her time. You know when you're on your way to a miracle, one of the things that the devil does is try to disgust you. Don't get disgusted. You're on the brink of one of the greatest miracles in your life! There are two things that the devil sends to mess up the saints. One is the spirit of vexation. He will try to vex you or make you disgusted. Stay focused. Your miracle is just around the corner so stay focused. So, the lady was taking her time and I was behind her. I was saying to myself, "Why don't you hurry up." She just took her time; she was in no hurry. This big, handsome, young, black man was behind me. He was so jolly and so happy, but I didn't know he was my miracle. He was flirting with all the girls. One of the girls said, "Hey Dude, you must be going to a party." He said, "Wait a minute, Sister. I'm a preacher." In my mind I said," Preacher?" It doesn't pay to judge anybody. When we walked inside, I said to him, "Are you a preacher?" He said, "Yes, I'm a preacher." I said, "Well, I'm Prophet DeCuir." He said, "Oh! You're the reason I'm saved." He said, "Sit down, Prophet!" I said, my seat is back there." He said, "Mine is up here. Sit up here with me and talk to me. He said, "Prophet, I was flirting with a girl when I got out of prison and she told me I needed to hear this tape. I didn't know anything about being saved, but she gave me your tape. The title of the tape was *A Change Is in Progress.*" He said, "Prophet, I heard that tape and I got saved. I wasn't even at church, but I got saved. I played that tape until it broke. Then I went to church and I told her I got saved and got filled with the Holy Ghost. I saw you on television before, but I've never met you. I'm so glad to meet you. I'd hear you on the radio and say, 'that man is my father.' My one desire was to meet my father."

We were having church right there and I said, "Man, I got to move," and he said, "Hold on before you move. I've got to give you an offering," and I needed an offering. He was writing a check and I wasn't praying. I was trying to see what he was writing. I said, he's giving me $50.00 and that's because I was going through something financially and I said, "Lord, have mercy." I was so glad to get $50.00, but then I looked again, and I saw that he gave me $500.00! I was so happy. He said, "I'll see you when we get to Fort Lauderdale." I said, "Okay." I went back there to my seat and a young black man was sitting next to me. He was about 22 years old and he said, "Hey Dude, what's the matter?" I said, "Man, how much is this check?" He said, "Dude, that check is $5,000.00" I said, "Are you reading right?" He said, "Dude, five-zero-zero-zero is $5,000.00, three zeros and .00 cents." I said, "Man, I got to get off the plane." The plane was backing out and he said, "Dude, I'll get you off." I said, "Man, you aren't the pilot. How are you going to get me off?" He said, "Lie down and I'm going to push the button to tell them you had a heart attack." I said, "You can't do that. I'm the prophet. That's a lie." He said, "You want to get off, don't you?" I said, "Man, I've got to wait." I stayed awake from Los Angeles to Fort Lauderdale. I looked at the check all night. When we got off the flight and we got downstairs, this guy came to the baggage claim. He had three limousines waiting on him and I said to one of the ladies who was with him, "What does he do?" She said, "He owns five *Taco Bells* and he's on his way now to buy two more." I want to tell you that for one year, that man sowed into my ministry. Sometimes, it was $1,200.00. Sometimes it was $2,000.00. God will bring some people out of nowhere to bless you. God will raise up people who will be compelled. They have to do it! They have to bless you. They have to help you. They have to give you the house. They have to give you the job. They have to give you the building. I prophesy the release on that building now! I prophesy for you to get up and walk in that building. I challenge you to get up and walk in now. Take the limits off. I hear the Lord saying, "Take off the limits; the building is yours! The daycare is yours!"

God said to Joshua, "*Moses is dead.*" Sometimes you have to just let some things be. He said, "*Now go over this Jordan.*" Did you notice that God didn't tell them how they were going to get over? He just said to go over this Jordan. You are worried about how you're going to get over, but you have to make a move. You can't be sitting down wondering how God is going to give you a house. You have to start seeing yourself in the house. People get quiet when you tell them they have to see it. You have to see a husband when you don't even have a boyfriend. Even if you don't have a sugar daddy or anything else, you have to see it. Stop saying, "I'm old." You aren't old. You're just right for a miracle.

The present generation is the Joshua generation. The Joshua generation is the generation that steps over and takes possession. They heard that prophecy all their lives and the old Israelites didn't take advantage of it. They just heard it. If you know what God has for you, you can't just talk. Have you ever heard the old folks say that talk is cheap, but money buys land? Talk is cheap, but a faith move is what brings you results. This is my season. I'm going to do like the Israelites and I'm going to get what's mine. The Lord said He's waiting on you.

The Lord told me to go to a restaurant when I didn't have enough money to even buy a steak. I said, I have enough to get some soup. I didn't know why I was in the restaurant, but I went to a place that they called the old folks' restaurant in California. I was there eating my soup and someone told a Hispanic lady, who could hardly speak English came by my church looking for me and they told her that I was at the restaurant. A little boy came in and said, "Mi Madre wants to see you." I said, "Where is your mom? Donde esta Madre?" He said, "She's in el coche." I said, "Donde esta el coche?" He said, "Outside." I went out there and he said, "Madre, here's the Padre." She said, "Padre! Padre! We've got to bless you!" She said, "I've got to do it today!" She said, "I heard you." I used to have a broadcast from 12:00 a.m. to 2:00 a.m. in the morning. She said, "I've got to bring you the dinero today." Madre pulled out an envelope while she was speaking in Spanish and praising God. I heard her say thank you Jesus and she said, "Mucho dinero para usted, Padre." I knew that it was for me. I took that envelope but I didn't want to open it in front of her. She praised God; I prayed for her. I waited for her to get in her car and pull off. When I opened that envelope there were fifty-one $100-dollar bills. You could tell that she had been saving them for years. God is going to release something for you that was stored up years ago.

I was in Detroit for 10 days in 2010. There was a man there who wouldn't come to church but came to the 12:00 p.m. service. He owed the Internal Revenue $25,000.00. I told him that I didn't know what he owed, but I said, "Why don't you give the Lord 10% of your bills." He looked at me as if to say, *oh crazy man, go sit down,* but his wife told him to do it. I want you to know he did it. He wrote a check for $3,500.00. His wife came to church that Sunday. She said, "Pastor, we gave the money on Tuesday and we got a letter yesterday from the Internal Revenue and they cancelled it."

# Chapter 22

# God Has a Plan for Your Life

There was a lady who, although she had an education, couldn't get a job anywhere. We had nine days of prayer and fasting, and in that fast we could only drink liquids (she needed to lose some weight anyway). She said I'm going to get a miracle, and she went on the fast. She had about $500.00 in the bank when she went on the fast. About two days before the fast she said, "Prophet, I gave everything I had." I said, "You didn't give everything you had." She said, "I have forty more dollars in the bank." I said, "Why don't you give that." She came back that Friday night and said, "God I sowed it all." She was shouting and I told her that the Lord said in seven days she was going to have that job.

She went to her sister's house, who had just met this guy who was trying to flirt. Her sister was an exceptionally good cook. She fried chicken like your mama used to fry; you know, like when you were a kid. No one's chicken tastes like mamas. The guy was one of the head supervisors for the Department of Motor Vehicles. He was sitting there, and as they were talking, she told him that she had been trying to get a job for three or four years. She said, "I want a job with the state." He said, "Have you applied?" She said, "No." He told her there was a job available because a lady in his office was resigning. She filled out the application. She's working there now. She's been over there now about two years and she said when he gets moved, she is going to take his place. She is going to become a supervisor. She's got about two more years to wait and he has already recommended her and he's training her to take his place. Fasting works!

A lady who lives in Atlanta and another lady who lives in Philadelphia heard me talking about this fast on the *Periscope* broadcast. They drove quite a distance to be here because they just wanted to be where the folks were fasting. The atmosphere changes when people start fasting. I'm believing God. I know that some of you are getting ready to experience some miracles as a result of this season of prayer and fasting.

A lady I knew, who lives in Atlanta now, said, "I just wanted to be around that atmosphere where people were fasting and praying." God spoke the other night and said, "Unusual miracles." If there ever was a time that you need to release your faith, it's during a season of prayer and fasting. I've been fasting for probably 40 years. Sometimes I go to the mountains and take prayer requests with me.

There was a man who had asked me if he could come on the fast. I was sitting in the church for a shut-in. You know we have to be careful who we tell to shut-in. We want to make sure the elevator is working on all floors. I said, "I guess you can." He said, "Where are you, Pastor?" "I want to lay right near you." I start wondering if he was alright or not.

I laid right behind the pulpit. I didn't know his name, but he would lay there every night across from me when I laid down, and I'd be praying. He kept praying one prayer, "God do it for me." I didn't know that man, but the doctor had told him he would only live for three months. His mother had told him to go down there and lay down near the prophet. When he left there seven days later, he was healed. He went back to the doctors and the doctor asked him what happened. He told him that he went on a fast. The doctor told him that everybody needs to go on that fast. It wasn't his faith that did it. It was his mother's faith. His mother had told him to go and lay down near the Prophet, and he was going to be healed.

Somebody's going to be healed. Your blood pressure is never ever going up again. Somebody needs to claim that right now. God is going to work unusual miracles.

I fasted and prayed. I have a son who is about 51 years old. He was a great football player. I just knew that I was going to be rich because I was waiting on him to sign a contract. But God's ways are not your ways. He had a scholarship to Wyoming University and we just knew he was going from there to one of those professional teams, but one day he knocked on my door. I said, "Son, what are you doing here?" He made up some excuse, and you know how the kids are; it's never them. He said, "Daddy, they kicked me off the team." The coach called me the next day. He said, "Your son is the best football player that I've ever had, but they spoil him and I'm not going to spoil him. He wants to come to practice when he gets ready and I said something to him, and he thought I was being a racist." He was in Wyoming, you know. So, they kicked him off the team. My son said, "Daddy, I'm going to go play for another team." But it wasn't in God's will. He tried everything. He tried out for the Raiders and we just knew he was going to get signed. The guy told him, "You got too much weight on you." We went to the gym and did everything, and he still didn't get picked up. He became so disturbed that he started dibbling and dabbling in drugs. He was staying with me, so I said, "Son, you can't have drugs in my house." He said, "Daddy, how do you know I have drugs?" I said, "Son, you have some drugs." He said, "There is nothing wrong with drugs." I said, "You know what I'm going to do? I'm going to tell you to get out of my house." He said, "I'm not going anywhere." I said, "You know what? You are going to eat football helmet for lunch!" I picked that helmet up and I said, "I'm going to shove this helmet down your esophagus." He said, "Daddy, you are saved." I said, "I know I am." He said, "Daddy, you are going to backslide. I said, "Okay I'm going to get reclaimed after you get finished eating this football helmet." My son is a big guy, but I said, "Now get out of here! Get out!" I found out later on, he would come back by the house at night and my kids would take him a plate of food. They were feeding him. But he went downhill.

I used to live in the mountains. I loved it because I like to go to the mountains to pray. He came by my house one day and it seemed like he was alright, but he had been out there on the street begging so that he could go buy some more drugs. I had to tell him again, "Son, there's a cliff in the back of my house and if you don't stop, you're going to be rolling down the side of the mountain." He would say, "I'm 50 years old and my daddy will whip me right now." Our parents told us that if you can't obey, you have to go, but we pray for our children. Some of you have some children; that's why God's got me telling this. Don't stop praying. Your faith is working.

For 15 years I fasted, and every fast, I put his name in the prayer box. One night the police called me and said,

"Reverend your son was almost killed." I remember we were praying, and I told God, don't let him get killed. He was throwing the policemen around like they were basketballs, and one policeman pulled a gun out and was going to kill him, but another policeman said that he wasn't worth it and pushed the gun back. You know what? That was prayer working. Your prayer is working. I want you to know, that boy got saved. God saved him. Last year he preached in my conference, Today he's a preacher because I had to fast and look beyond what I saw and what I heard.

Mark 11:22 says, *"And Jesus answered and said unto them, have faith in God."* Jesus is telling you today, have faith in God. Not faith in what you see. Not what you're trying to understand. Faith is not limited to your sight nor your understanding. Have you ever looked at something and said, "How can God do this?" It is none of your business how He's going to fix it; just know He's going to fix it. You have to look at that house and say I know He's going to give me that house. You have to look in that mirror and see yourself, if you're not married, and tell yourself honey bunny is coming. I don't know where he's coming from. I don't know his name, but I'm faithful and I believe God, and God is going to send me a husband, and when God sends him, he's not going to be a problem. You're not going to have to give him Prozac every morning to wake up and Prozac to go to work. God's not going to send you a reject either. He's going to send you somebody who's going to stand by you. You have to tell yourself, "I'm getting married."

I know a woman who told herself that she was getting married. She had no boyfriend and no sugar daddy. She had nobody cutting the lawn, but she was saying, "That's my yard man."

As I was preaching in Detroit, I said, "You know that isn't your yard man. He's cutting more than grass. Are you hearing me?" I didn't know what I was talking about. I was just talking. Afterwards, a mother came up crying, and said, "Pastor, I want to marry him." His name was Bo. "I want to marry him, but we're both on Social Security and if we get married, Pastor, God understands. I know He does. I want to do right." She said, "You know, Bo is not my yard man. He's really my boyfriend, and you told everything today." I said, "Mother, I didn't tell anything." She said, "But the Holy Ghost did." The Holy Ghost will expose you. She said, "I don't want to go to hell, Prophet, but I need my little check." She said, "What do I do?" I said, "Well Mother, you and Bo are going to have to stop. You have to go get married." She said, "Why? I don't want Bo to go; I love him." You could feel that mother's love too. I said, "Well

Mother, you have to go get married. Release your faith. God is going to work a miracle."

So, they got married and Mother was still talking about not knowing what she was going to do. So, I went back, and she said, "Prophet, I got married and we are barely making it, but I sure feel good doing it right." I went to church at the 12:00 p.m. service and I said, "Mother, the Lord said give everything in your purse." She looked at Bo and Bo said, "Give it." She had about $12.00, and she looked at Bo and said, "Bo, do you have some more money?" He said, "I have $5.00. Give everything in your purse." Mother poured it out. God's got a miracle already set up. Mother gave that money on Tuesday and she came back Thursday. She said, "I gave all my money and my daughter came by the house this morning and gave me $50.00" The Holy Ghost told me to tell her that God wasn't through. Mother gave $40.00 of that money.

Her son-in-law works for a millionaire in Detroit and all he and his wife do is travel. The man called her son-in-law in and said, "Listen, do you know of some older people?" Remember now, they lost their income when they got married. At first the son-in-law couldn't think of anything, but then he said, "Wait a minute, my wife's Mother." He said, "I need some old people. They don't have to do anything but stay on the property. They don't have to buy any food. They don't have to pay light bills. They don't have to do anything and we're going to pay them $2,000.00 a month to stay on the property." That's double the money that both of them were receiving, and they don't have to buy groceries; they just stay there while the couple travel, and when they come back, Mother and Bo can just stay there. The couple gave them a credit card so that they can go buy groceries and whatever they want to eat. God's got something already set up for you, but you're around here worried.

Mother and Bo are in Detroit right now. They're over there at that man's house more than they are at their own house and they get paid $2,000.00 every month. They don't have to clean the house. They're getting paid for watching the house. They have a garden. The millionaires live over there. They have a security guard to go around and watch all the houses, but they wanted somebody on the property. They have a dog, a big old Rottweiler. Mother has almost taught the dog how to pray. The dog's named Chi-Chi. Mother says, "Stop barking, I'm praying." She said when she gets to praying, old Chi-Chi goes over there and sits down.

God's got something set up for you and it's getting ready to happen! I believe God! I remember the song they used to sing, *Something good is going to happen to you this very day.'* God told me to tell you that He's got something set up for you and it's getting ready to manifest. Forget those things that are behind. What's done is already done. Stop reliving it. The man is gone and he is never coming back. He's over there with Lulabelle and you're over here depressed. He isn't depressed over there with Lulu. Leave him over there. I said that in Philadelphia one time. I said everybody go and to tell somebody that he isn't coming back. A woman said, "Prophet, it hit me in the head that the one I had wasn't coming back." God blessed her. Some stuff you've just got to release. God is writing new history about you anyway. Turn the page and read that new history.

Mark 11:22 says, *"Jesus answering said unto them have faith in God."* Now according to the Bible, God has given every man and every woman faith. I've got faith and mine is working. The Lord said to tell someone that he's opening up a new position. It's going to be like your old business but you're going to be one of God's entrepreneurs on another level, which most of our people don't ever get to.

The Lord said it's going to be like you will have your own business. God is going to connect you. There's a millionaire coming out of somewhere; don't let anybody take advantage of you. Find yourself a good lawyer because there's going to be so much money involved. The Lord will cover you. The Lord will protect you. The Lord will give people to help you. There will be so many people working with you. I see people working. I see a marketing team. Something is going to happen for you over across the water. It's going to be an overseas connection.

Isn't God something? He can send encourage you wherever you are. God is doing that kind of stuff. We're going to see this in the church, such a transfer of wealth. He's going to give people ideas and inventions. We're going to see corporations bringing wealth to the people of God.

There was a lady in California who had four different marriages fall apart. You know when that kind of stuff happens to you, you're just down. I went over one day and hit her on the head, not hard. I said, "Wake up, rich woman." She looked around and told the lady next to her, "He must be talking about you." I said, "You have such a love for old people." She started crying and I said, "You just love old people and your love for old people is going to make you rich." She said, "I don't know why, but I do love old people." I said, "Do what God tells you to do. Pray for seven days and whatever God tells you to do, do it." She prayed. There was an older lady living down the street, and one day the lady's daughter called her and said, "Will you fix dinner for Mamma every day?" She said, "Yeah." She would pick the lady up and bring her down to her house.

The next thing you know, she had two ladies there. She said she was laying in the bed and the Lord said to open up a daycare for senior citizens. She said, "Lord, I don't have any money." Don't be so quick to say what you don't have. If you have the idea and the faith, God's got the money. Stop worrying about money. She was driving down the street when she saw a building that had been empty for three years. She found the owners of the building. They lived in San Marino, California, where nothing but filthy rich people lived. She went to the house and the people in the neighborhood saw her coming. She hadn't dressed up. She just had on blue jeans and a hat. The lady was scared to open the door, but she finally opened it. She told the lady, "Ma'am, I'm a Christian. I didn't come to bother anything." The lady said, "Forgive me, I was apprehensive to see somebody Black coming with a hat on." She said, "I understand that there is a building that belongs to you." She said, "Yes it does, and we can't rent it. We've been trying to rent it for three years." She couldn't rent it because God was holding it for her. There's some stuff that God is holding for you and all you're going to have to do is show up.

When she got through talking to that lady and telling her that she wanted to keep senior citizens, the lady said, "You know the rent is $3,000.00 a month." She never told the lady she didn't have any money. Keep those words out of your mouth: 'I don't have any money.' The lady said, "What all are you going to need?" She said, "Well, I'm going to need couches. I'll need maybe one or two beds." She said, "Maybe I'll need ten beds for if they want to take a break during the day." She said she didn't know why she told the woman everything that she needed. She said, "I need a stove and five or six of those big screen TVs." The lady called her brother, who owned the biggest furniture store in town, and gave him her name, and told him that she was coming down. "Give her whatever she needs," she said. They still hadn't talked about the rent. She got a building full of everything she needed. When the lady's husband came home, she told him, "This lady is renting our building." She was speaking faith. She told him what she wanted to do, and her vision, and the man said, "Oh, that's wonderful. Since you're doing that for the older people, we're going to give you six months free rent and we're going to pay the water bill, the light bill, and pay everything." Somebody is looking for you; they've already been programmed to bless you.

You've heard the story of Elijah where God told him to go down to the brook Cherith and he said to Elijah, I have commanded the ravens to feed you there. Somebody's under command. They may not want to do it, but they've got to do it. The raven is nothing but a buzzard, and he doesn't give anything to anybody. But God reprogrammed him. God is reprogramming somebody to bless you. Somebody's going to be reprogrammed when you get to the car lot. They have to do it. They might not want to do it, but they have to do it. Somebody is reprogrammed when they see you coming. When you go get your house, they're reprogrammed. They're selling it for $50,000.00, but when you get there, God's going to make them cut it down. They're reprogrammed to help you. They have to do it. You're going to have that building. You're going to have that business. Open your mouth and say, "I'm going to have it now." Have faith in God. If you want to get what God's got for you, you have to have faith in God. You have to know that God said it.

Somebody is going to give me a building. I want to build hotel apartments. I don't want a cabin. I want people coming to make reservations. I have to make it like you are at the Holiday Inn. I believe somebody is going to give me the land. Somebody's going to give me the building. I'm going to somebody's furniture stores, and I want to them to furnish it. When you come in there, I want the spirit of peace to overtake you. When you come on the grounds, praise music is coming up out of the ground. When you are walking to your room, you'll hear praise music. When you go outside, walking at night, all you're going to hear is praise music. Somebody is going to do it. Somebody is going to give me that land. People ask me where it's going to be. And I said I don't know. I believe it by faith. My faith is working.

For years, since they were kids, my kids have been hearing me talk about the prayer center, But now they've got it. They're saying Daddy's going to build a prayer center. People thought I stepped down from being a pastor. I turned the church over. My kids say Daddy didn't step down to retire; he stepped down to build the world's prayer center, where for 24-hours, people are praying. If you watch me on *Facebook* you will see I have people now, taking an hour to pray. We're going to have twenty-four people praying around the clock with each person taking an hour. For 90 days we're praying for the nation. The next thing we're praying for is the preachers, and next, for our children, for God to cover and protect them. Then we're praying for God to cover the saints and keep them from all of these diseases that are trying to attack our bodies.

There's a mother I know, who was getting ready to go to heaven. Sometimes when I'd go to church at 12:00 p.m. when I was a pastoring, I would sit down and begin to talk. A boy told me about 15 years ago, "Prophet, you've preached long enough get a chair. I didn't pay him any mind because I still thought I was young and all that stuff. But since that time, sometimes I do get a chair. He was right.

Mother had cancer and they said she wouldn't live six months. I read one scripture to Mother. You would be surprised at what can happen when you catch a hold to the Word and watch God move in your life. I read Psalm 118:17, and Mother caught that thing. It says, *"I shall live and not die."* Mother started saying that, and she isn't dead yet! She was supposed to die, and it's been more than three years and Mother is still living because her faith connected to the Word.

I learned the power of the Word when I was about 29 years old. I went to church with my son (you know, the one who I later almost made eat helmet for dinner), who was a baby. I saw a Caucasian man in the street and said to my son's mother that the man was hungry. I said, "The Lord said for us to take the man home and feed him, and that He would meet our needs." So, she called my mama and said, "Mama, Rogers is saying the Lord said for us to take this man in the house and feed him and let him stay overnight." My mamma said, "Baby you know Rogers used to do it to me. He would bring children home and say, 'Mama, we have to feed these children.'

When I was a child, I used to go through the neighborhood and if any kids were hungry, I'd tell them to come to my house. Sometimes children would eat up all the food and my mama would say, "What are you going to eat?" I was sitting there, knowing they were hungry, and she would say, "Go in the kitchen and find yourself something." I would go make myself a peanut butter sandwich or jam sandwich (but there was no jam; it was two pieces of bread jammed together with mayonnaise).

I remembered that, and I had just gone to church, and the preacher preached that my God shall supply. We fed the man, we prayed for him, and we put him on our couch since we only had one bedroom. He got up the next morning, thanked us, and went on his way. The next day my brother-in-law came by. He said, "I want to give you $50.00." We only had $6.00. The next morning the same white man knocked on our door with a suit on and a pair of glasses. He said, "You know, I was out there, but I wasn't a bum. Somebody stole my car and took my money, but this morning they got my car back. He said, "In my car was $10,000.00. It wasn't in my glove compartment, but I had it in the back in the trunk behind the tire in a special place. I came back to bless you." Of course, we didn't know anything about faith then. We were just kids. He gave us seven $100-dollar bills. God has somebody set up. God has somebody, who when you meet that somebody, they've already been programmed to bless you, and they have to do it!

Take the Limits off Your Faith!

# Author's Biographical Sketch

Prophet Rogers G. Decuir is a renowned conference host, teacher, preacher, workshop presenter, evangelist, and prophet, flowing in the five-fold ministry gifts. Because of his insight, wisdom, and discernment, Prophet DeCuir has been a spiritual father to many across this nation. He has mentored and guided many sons and daughters in the ministry, and has equipped them to be anointed, effective, and fruitful spiritual leaders. He has traveled throughout the country hosting revivals, helping to launch new churches, and assisting established churches and pastors in developing and strengthening their ministries.

Today Prophet DeCuir reaches thousands by way of radio and television. When asked by young ministers what has helped him to endure, he simply replies "prayer, fasting, holy living, and a total commitment to God and the assignment that He has given me."

Prophet DeCuir has a reputation for his perseverance, consistency, and love. He has always been faithful to his calling and to the needs of his church and community.

Prophet Rogers G. DeCuir has been preaching the gospel of our Lord and Savior Jesus Christ for over 70 years. He is the founder and overseer of Holy Deliverance Pentecostal Church in Pasadena, California, where he pastored for over 50 years. Prophet DeCuir is known for leading his church and the people of God in periods of prayer and fasting.

# Author's Contact Information

Email: pastordecuir@gmail

Facebook: Rogers G DeCuir

Mailing Address: P.O. Box 50002, Pasadena, CA 91115

Phone: (626)303-3690

Booking Information: provisionghmfm@yahoo.com

Website: http://www.prophetdecuir.org

Made in USA - Crawfordsville, IN
51774_9780578654782
12.21.2020 1756